Memories of Lynn
(1950 to 1975)

Marks & Spencer Christmas Party
Dukes Head 1965

Tricky Sam Publishing

Introduction

In the book a very small number of photos have appeared in other publications but I felt their inclusion here was necessary for the continuity of the book.

A special thanks to all the staff at the Norfolk County Council Library & Information Service, King's Lynn for all their help to the author, to Colin Bailey of Fraser Dawbarns for his legal expertise, John Allen for his help on layout & proof reading, Yvonne at Clanpress, Wilson & Betts for their continued support, David Sharp of Active Life Physiotherapy, Tony at The Record Shop and to Janet for her cover design and advice.

The copyright of photographs from the Lynn News, West Norfolk Borough Council and the Eastern Daily Press is acknowledged and gratefully appreciated.

Acknowledgements

John Allen	Robin Edwards	Colin Johnson	Kathleen Reed	Pat Thorpe
Tony & Ann Allen	Diane Engledow	Jean Judge	Arthur Richardson	Peter Todhunter
June Backmeier	Brian Fisher	Jo Land	Terry Rose	Margaret Toll
Pat Barnard	Alan Fry	Nora Langley	Jim Rudley	Bernie Towler
Alan & Doreen Booth	Lynda Fuller	Mary Loasby	St Edmunds School	Jim Tuck
Bill Booth	Colin Fysh	Pat Long	Mick Sayer	Bill Turner
Roger Booth	Dick Goodchild	Amanda Lovejoy	Michael & Susan Sexton	Wendy Twite
Ron Bowyer	Bill Graver	Rene Lusher	Linda & Rod Sheen	Irene Twyman
Sheila Broughton	Paddy Green	Eddie Lyon	Rod Shirley	Jennifer Twyman
Ray Bullock	Pat Green	Marion McNulty	Beryl Sleight	Colin Venemore
Sue Carter	Gerald Groom	Pete & Mina Mott	Steve & Trudi Smalls	June Walker
Neville Carter	Ann Hall	Barbara Neep	Ian Smith	Dennis & Shirley Walker
Gill Coleman	Pauline Heil	Teresa Nicholls	Ken & Jill Smith	Sue Ward
Doug Crisp	Rosemary Huggins	Mandy Nixon	Andrew Stevenson	John Webber
Judy & Charlie Curtis	Joan Jarvis	Keith Nurse	Geoff Stinton	Anne Woodward
Liz Dyer	Christine Johnson	Maureen Plowright	Richard Taylor	David Wright

Copyright © Bob Booth 2009

First Printed 2009

Published by Tricky Sam Publishing (trickysampublishing@tiscali.co.uk)

Printed by Clanpress, King's Lynn
Tel: 01553 772737   Email: john@clanpress.co.uk

All rights reserved.
No part of this publication may be reproduced in any form without prior permission from the publisher.

TOP LEFT: 1950 Robin Edwards shows his catch from the Gaywood river by the 'Stone Bridge' to (*left to right*): ?Akers, Mel Greenacre, Rex Hendry, Paul Anderson & J Greenacre.

TOP RIGHT: Robin Edwards and friends paddle down the Gaywood river on their home-made raft in 1952.

LEFT: Billy Graver watches the trains from the road bridge over South Lynn station circa 1960.

BELOW LEFT: 1951 Gaywood Park Boys visit the Festival of Britain.

BELOW RIGHT: 1955. 1^d for the Guy!
From left to right: David Wakeling, John Cork, the Guy (Gerry Foreman) and Terry Rose try collecting down a very quiet London Road.

BOTTOM LEFT: In 1948 Gaywood Park Boys take a day out at London Zoo.

3

The early 1960s. The Fisherman's Arms is at 36, Pilot Street and further down was the Fisherman's Return (closed February 1962) and the Tilden Smith (closed in November 1974).
The Fisherman's Return and the Tilden Smith were separated by the railway crossing to the docks. The Tilden Smith later re-opened as The Retreat.

TOP: A view of the new Fisherman's Arms from Pilot Street. By the mid 1960s the Fisherman's Arms had been demolished and rebuilt in a slightly different position on the new John Kennedy Way.

ABOVE: Pilot Street in 1958 looking towards Hextable Road. At this time the Fisherman's Arms would be somewhere opposite the lorry standing outside Southall's shoe factory (originally St Nicholas School).

ABOVE LEFT: Lin-can staff wait on London Road for transport to West Lynn.
ABOVE RIGHT: Ron Bowyer & Harold Fisher wearing new hats and now classed as 'Junior Postmen' instead of 'Telegram Boys' circa 1950.

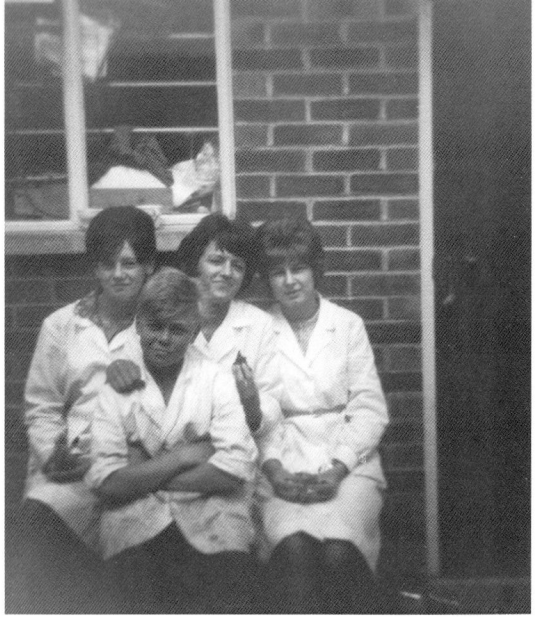

MIDDLE LEFT: April 1959. Mat making and dredging on the river bank - the railway bridge now redundant following the M&GN closure in February 1959 is in the background. Second right in the picture is Bill Loasby.
MIDDLE RIGHT: Staff of the Seabank Co-op take a tea break in the back yard in 1963. Left to right: Pat Lockley, Robert 'Butch' West, Josephine Auker & Ann Trusler. Butch delivered groceries on his trade bike after school.

BOTTOM LEFT: Ladyman's waitresses take a break on the fire escape in the early 1950s. The group (from the top): Eileen, Pam, Millie, ?, Joan Doughty & Hilda.

BOTTOM RIGHT: Circa 1950. Michael Irwin and Bob 'Minnie' Mason on their GPO bikes behind the Sorting Office, Baxter's Plain. Inspector Freeman sees them off.

TOP RIGHT:
Training at Lynn Regis Boxing Club in 1953.

The gym was at the back of St George's Guildhall, King Street.

Peter Sorenson demonstrates the straight left to:
Left to right: Terry Chilvers, Charlie Curtis and Jimmy Larkman.

The club was run by local ship's chandler Tom Reynolds.

RIGHT: The King's Lynn Weightlifting & Body Building Club met weekly at the Red Barn, The Guildhall of St George. Here, in December 1958, Dennis Walker demonstrates 'The Squat'. Club members looking on include: Fred Hall, Fred Harvey, Wally Warnes, Brian Van Pelt, Brian Whomes, Ted Rogers and Brian Williamson - along with the Mayor, Mr AJ Barker, Deputy Mayor, Mr EA Anderson (dark suit) and Mr J Cuthbert (club secretary).

BOTTOM RIGHT:
The Youth Club, Tower Street 1953. Judo training for the girls - the art of self defence.
The local police had organised a one-off class.

The Youth Club was very popular and gave the youth of the day somewhere to go in the evening.

It was demolished by 1972 when the access road Regent Way was built.

TOP: Class 1B Gaywood Park Girls in 1956
Back row (left to right): Adrienne Daws, Christine Short, Shirley Fox, Kathleen Dewson, Janet Wilson, Kathleen Ross, Jill Day, Doreen Belcher, Sandra Ormarod, Glenda Wagg.
Middle Row: Janet Bush, Judith Ryan, Eve Morley, Sandra Fysh, Diane Holland, Linda Brock, Shirley Youngs, Jean Delaney, Diane Baker, Betty Kent, Christine Bolton.
Front row: Mary Hardy, Margaret Walker, Vera Wakefield, Diane Reed, Linda Toll, Miss Gittens, Marion Kendle, Maureen Humm, Daphne Whitting, Marie Whitting, Valerie Smith.

MIDDLE LEFT: December 1954. Iolanthe at the St George's Guildhall - a joint production by the High School and the Grammar School.
This did not receive a very favourable review in the local paper (*'plenty of enthusiasm but lack of artistry with weak singing from the tenors'*)!

LEFT:
Rosebery Avenue Primary School at the time of the Coronation in 1953.

Pupils include: Patricia Bodsworth, Margaret Norton, Jane Barrett, Diana Back, Roger Booth, Jonathan Robbins, David Ballard, Louis Donald, David Fox, Paul Anderson, Geoffrey Suiter, Lillian Spitz, Andrew Bates, Andrew Adkins.

The teacher in the middle at the back is Mrs Smeed.

RIGHT: Celebrating the opening of the new bar at the Workers Club, Church Street. in 1950 with a game of billiards.

Charlie Hornigold (club chairman) breaks watched by Jack Lambert.

LEFT:
Workers Club children's Christmas party in 1951.

BELOW:1953
A British Legion children's party at Priory Hall, Priory Lane.
Among those present were: Mrs Birdseye, Grace Edgley, Margaret Bullen, Rosie Neal, Barbara Lord, Kathleen Ross, Pat Roberts, Jenny Birdseye, Ann Ross, John Neal, Colin Loasby, Mrs Loasby.

TOP LEFT:
Saturday Market Place on Sunday 17th September 1963.

The march-past of contingents following the Battle of Britain Commemoration at St Margaret's Church.

Receiving the salute is the Mayor (Alderman Albert Bacon) and other dignitaries including the Battle of Britain queen (Kathleen Hubbard).

LEFT:
Saturday Market Place, December 1969.
No. 7 Saturday Market Place is Maudes, No. 6 is Priors, No. 5 was Duke of Fife, No. 4 Eva Baird (antiques) No. 3 Barringtons (florists), No. 2 is empty (Barretts laundry was here but had vacated the property a year or two before) and No. 1 is Courts (house furnishers).

RIGHT:
Saturday Market Place in September 1958 looking west.
From the right in the picture: Miss Gertrude Bullen (confectioner & St Margaret's Café), Duke of Fife (public house), EH Prior (butcher), Maudes (credit draper & outfitter). The building on the corner is 1 High Street.

Highgate in the mid 1950s
TOP: Front Row, Highgate.
ABOVE: Double Row, Highgate.

By the mid 1950s it was decided that the living conditions in Highgate were not acceptable. The front page of the Lynn News proclaimed that:
'*Double Row days are numbered*'.
The pictures on this page chart Norman Barger Jones (Additional Sanitary Inspector for the Council) making notes on the state of properties in Highgate.

In March 1959 the first plans were approved for the new development.

MIDDLE RIGHT: Front Row. Norman Jones makes notes while the milkman's delivery trike stands ready for the next customer.

BOTTOM RIGHT: Front Row. Cyclists head for Gaywood Road, with a backward glance from Mr Jones.

11

Frederick Savage started his own business in St Nicholas Street (St Nicholas Iron Works) after working for several firms in Norfolk. He started manufacturing fairground rides (Dobby Horses). In 1873 a new St Nicholas Ironworks was built in Estuary Road. By 1874 he had built a large house (BELOW) for himself and Mrs Savage. He also built 18 houses in George Street and 14 houses on the north side of Gaywood Road. He died in 1897 and was succeeded by his two sons. In 1910 the business was declared bankrupt owing to the two sons (who were rather fond of women and drink) extending too much credit to roundabout owners. A consortium of local businessmen bought the company which then ran until 1973 when the company ceased trading. Savages are best remembered for fairground rides and agricultural machinery.

TOP LEFT: George (pattern maker &wood turner) & Victor (carpenter) Walker show some of their work.
TOP RIGHT: A completed ride. Mr Johnson (works manager) on the left. MIDDLE LEFT: George Walker at his bench in the carpentry shop. MIDDLE RIGHT: The 'saw doctor' Wilfred Walker.
RIGHT: Plaque (photographed in 2009) on the north side of Gaywood Road showing the location of a row of houses built by Mr Savage for his employees

TOP: 1962. Estuary Road looking from the front of Savages towards the Victoria pub. The left turn to Loke Road can be seen just before the pub.
MIDDLE: 1962. A view from Loke Road - turn right for Savages and the Fisher Fleet. The cranes on the Alexandra Dock can be seen.
BOTTOM LEFT: A view down Loke Road, looking east, in 1965. A Ford Zephyr stands outside DF Booth (turf commission agents). This Ford model cost nearly twice the price of a Ford Anglia - does it belong to the bookie or a lucky punter?
BOTTOM RIGHT: The Bentinck pub in 1965 - a favourite with the fishing community. To the left of the pub is Cresswell Street.

ABOVE: Class 3A Gaywood Park in 1954.
Back row (left to right): Rosalyn Finney, Brenda Tooke, Pauline Myers, Barbara Turville, Linda Heath.
Middle row: Yvonne Hall, Diane Howlett, Prunella Bensley, Julie Harper, Angela Shepherd, Jill Moore, Margaret Towler, Jacqueline Elsdon, Valerie Howlett, Meryn Haines, Ruth Castleton, Sylvia Graver, Doreen White, Barbara Bretton.
Front row: Valerie Simmonds, Mary Massen, Diana Starling, Wendy Merrison, June Muir, Pamela Stebbing, Kathleen Roy, Miss Draper, Brenda Snelling, Maureen Bowman, Angela Courtman, Beryl Hudson, Olive Carter, Marie Carter, Maureen Kirk.

LEFT: King's Lynn Technical College, Hospital Walk in 1954. Engineering, Domestic Science & Commerce students are photographed outside the front of the building.

BOTTOM: St James Primary school Christmas Concert at St Margaret's Church in December 1955.

LEFT: 1962. Four contestants in a fancy dress competition at Lynn Youth Centre Christmas dance.
Tony Pitt and Pat Lemon (as Black and White Minstrels), David Cawston (as a gypsy pedlar) and Mrs K Davis (as a Chinese girl). The judges, Mr & Mrs Goldsworthy, did not give prizes for the best two entries. Instead they gave £1 apiece to all who took part.

BELOW: Pupils of Miss Phyllis Pickering's Royal Borough School of Dancing in the mid 1950s. This was at 27, Railway Road.

ABOVE LEFT: 1952 'When we are Married'. A comedy by The King's Lynn Players at the Pilot.

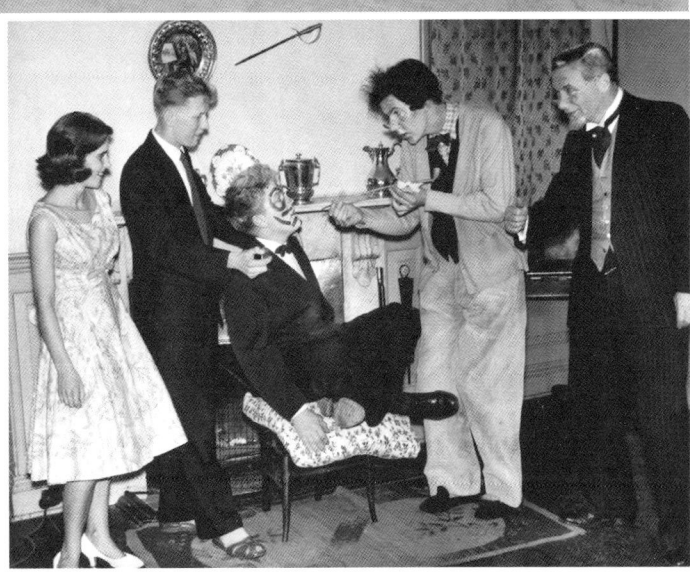

ABOVE RIGHT: 1959 'Bell, Book and Candle'. The King's Lynn Players perform another comedy at The Guildhall.

1953 Coronation Year celebrations.
TOP: Parkway, Gaywood. Roy Johnson (bottom right in picture), a well known local pianist entertains the children with his accordion.

RIGHT: Hextable Road. The passage between Lansdowne Street & Birchwood Street is converted into a 'Coronation grotto'.

FAR RIGHT: Paddy & Kate Mears driving a Briton 'Stuart' (built in Wolverhampton c1907) round the Tuesday Market Place. The car had been rescued in a derelict state from Taylor's orchard in Tennyson Avenue.

RIGHT: Street party at Harecroft Gardens, (Loke Road).
Back row (left to right): Mrs Willot, Barry Gardiner, Mary Harrod, Margaret Fenton, Barry Bunton, ?, Michael Cordery, Mrs Harrod, Sylvia Fisher.
Third row: Colin Goodson, Cynthia Land, Michael Sexton, Andrew Bullen. *Second row:* Janet Wilson, ?, Richard Sexton, Annette Willot, Mrs Fisher, ?, Christine Fenton, Peter Williams, ?
Front row: Michael Jessop, ?, ?, Lesley Main, Robert Williams, ?, Brian Thurley, ?.

ABOVE: Gaywood Park Girls, 1955. *Left to right:* Rose Luther, Christine Moore, Ann Dowdney, Brenda Wilson, ?, ?, Pat Jolley, Miss Dunwoody, Joan Batterham, Mary Harris, Mary Harrod, Joyce Bain, Brenda Seaman, Jane Shortis, ?

MIDDLE LEFT: St James Primary Girls School (Paxton Terrace) in 1957.

BOTTOM: Alderman Catleugh, 1958/9. *Back row (left to right):* Ginny Bush, Gill Stebbings, Mary Briston, Bronka Kanoska, Pat Long, Jean Clark, Margaret Mitchell, Valerie Sadler, Pamela Cawston, *Front row* Margaret Lusher, June Collins, Gillian Reeve, Suzette Chapman, Sylvia Gates, Jennifer Barnes, Margaret Boughen, Elsie Ford, Jennifer Quince.

St. Edmund's School

ABOVE: 1956. St. Edmund's Junior School, Estuary Road. Adjoining the Junior School was St. Edmund's Infants' School.

RIGHT: Miss FM Oliver (second from left), Headmistress, and Miss E Chase welcome some of the first children to be enrolled at the new North Lynn Infant's School (St. Edmund's) in September 1953. In the background is the assembly hall.

BELOW LEFT: Children wait on the stairs of St. George's Guildhall in 1957.

BELOW RIGHT: On 23rd June 1969 Lynn's first pedestrian subway opens to allow the children of St. Edmund's to safely reach school by going under the new northern ring road (when finished) connecting Estuary Road, North Lynn with South Wootton.

TOP: Peter Guest garage at 123/125, Wootton Road in 1961.

ABOVE: In 1962 an AA man has stopped at 341, Wootton Road - CA Thurston's café although it was usually referred to as Murrell's after Mrs Sophia Murrell who had been the previous owner (then listed as 'refreshment rooms'). Between Blakes & the Murrell's was Malt Row, a terrace of 13 houses running at 90° to the road.

BOTTOM LEFT: 1962. Blake Brothers (cycle dealers) at 347, Wootton Road. There was also a blacksmiths at the back operated by Ernest Blake. Beyond is the New Inn.

TOP: 1960. 30, Wootton Road. Bensleys of Gaywood Ltd (radio & TV) also served petrol.

RIGHT: 1956. 281, Wootton Road. Variously owned by Frederick Ashton (tobacconist & newsagent)), Douglas Mears (general store) and Wilkinson & Hill (shopkeepers) between the mid to late 1950s. It became known as Mill Stores.
Not long after this photo was taken the obsolete petrol pumps were removed.

BOTTOM: 1959. 301, Wootton Road. Empire Garage (Triumph, Standard & Volkswagen dealers).
Just beyond the garage between the two bungalows is Empire Avenue.

TOP: A view up Wootton Road in the early 1960s. The road to the left is Marsh Lane and the water tower on the right supplies Burn's nursery. To the right of the camera is the Eastern Electricity Board and behind is the Stone Bridge.

LEFT: 1966. The gap between 218 and 224, Wootton Road was to be the entrance to the new Reffley Estate (Fenland Road).
BOTTOM LEFT & RIGHT: Reffley Temple & Reffley Spring in 1970. The temple was built in the 17th century as a meeting place for Royalists who were anti-parliamentarians. It was more of a boozers club - the traditional drink was punch made using the spring water.
Only Norfolk born men could join.

ABOVE LEFT: King Edward V11 School under 13 football team of 1968/69.

ABOVE RIGHT: Gaywood Park Girls, 1958. Sadie Twite leads Maureen Skipper in the senior hurdles race.

BELOW LEFT: The swimmers ready for the Ouse annual championship swim in the late 1950s outside the Conservancy Board on Common Staith Quay.
Left to right: Judy Richardson, Christine Proctor, ?, Clarice Howard, Diana Howell, Joan Bailey, Margaret Proctor.

BELOW RIGHT: 1958. High School Hockey team.

BOTTOM: The Grammar School 'open' mile start in 1955. The winner was Peter Wormall in a time of 4m 50s.

Behind the cricket pavilion is the Hunstanton railway line and, beyond that, Gaywood Park.

TOP LEFT: 1955. Friars Street from South Lynn Plain looking south. To the right of the camera is Whitefriars & Gladstone Roads.
The building on the left was the Goat Inn - demolished 2 years after this picture was taken.
The pub dated from 1695 although at least one window was from the 15th century. The last drinks were served in 1912.

ABOVE LEFT & RIGHT: The Friars (from All Saints Street) in 1959. In the left hand picture the gate to the Carmelite or White Friars monastery can be seen. The White Friars were very austere - observing silence and even sleeping in their coffins!
The building on the left of both pictures is part of the Bestyett mineral works.
In the right hand picture can be seen a sign to the 'Boal Quay Wharfingers' or wharf owners.

LEFT: Bestyett Mineral Water also in 1959.
In 1952/3 one of my after-school jobs working for 'Doc' Russell Lankshear was to deliver preservative, which had been prepared in his lab in Union Street, to Bestyett for their soft drinks.

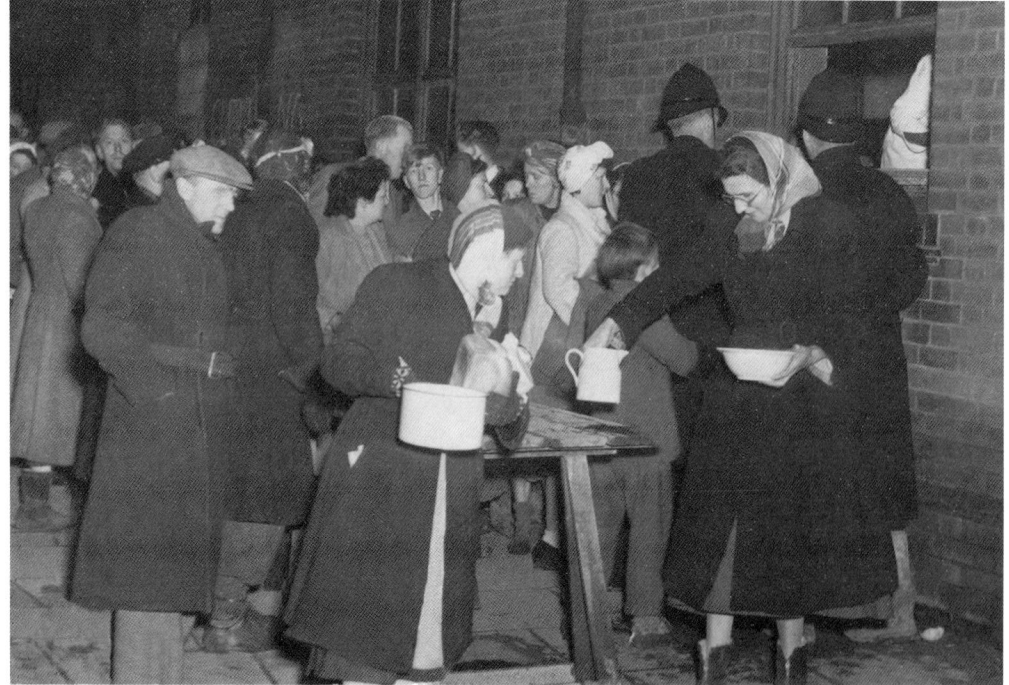

TOP LEFT: South Lynn caught the worst of the 31st January 1953 floods - by the next day food and hot drink had been organised in true old-fashioned British spirit.
TOP RIGHT: Bailing out in Purfleet Street.
MIDDLE LEFT: South Lynn station the day after the floods.
MIDDLE RIGHT: Another make-shift kitchen is set up. The Queen and the mayor Mr Freestone (fourth from right, holding hat) are in attendance.  
BOTTOM LEFT: A silent tribute at The Walks on the following Saturday.
BOTTOM RIGHT: Red Cross to the rescue! A cutting from the Lynn News.

Red Cross to the rescue

RED CROSS Driver Nurse carries Miss Lyons across flooded London Road—and the situation is made light of with a smile.

24

TOP: Bottling milk at Seaman's Dairy on Wootton Road (next to the Eastern Electricity Board) in 1958. On the right Wendy Twite collects bottles from the line.

MIDDLE LEFT: Lynn Drawing office in 1957 at Clifton House. *Left to right*: Don Colquhoun, John Randall (Chief Assistant), Barry Hall, Bob Hall, Alan Dawes.

MIDDLE RIGHT: 1953. A group of National Servicemen from the Lynn area pose at Bude. With the end of the war it was decided to introduce conscription (or national service) to help maintain world peace. Those eligible received a medical (sometimes embarrassing when asked to drop your trousers and cough for a lady doctor). A few weeks later a brown envelope would arrive and you would then report to an Army/RAF base for 10 weeks training, followed by a two year stint, before returning to a normal life and career - unless you liked it enough to 'sign on'.

BOTTOM RIGHT: 1958 Telephone Exchange. An introduction to STD (standard telephone dialling). *Left to right*: Joan Diaper, Wendy Porter, Alan Sable (supervisor), Barbara Manning, Dulcie Garner, ?Spooner, ?.

Gaywood Park Girls Sports Day

ABOVE 1956 Members of Balmoral House cheer on their fellow house members.

RIGHT: 1956. An action photo of the shot putt.

LEFT: The hurdles race in 1957.

LEFT: 1957. The winners of the house shield, Marlborough House, pose for the camera. The shield had been presented by Mr JH Catleugh (the chairman of the school governors). Marlborough were clear winners attaining 76½, 14 more than their nearest rivals Glamis.

ABOVE: Empire Day celebrations at St James' Girls (Paxton Terrace) in the early 1950s. Empire Day was devised at the beginning of the 20th century as a means of training school children in good citizenship. The day consisted of showing themes of British history and life in the British Empire.

BOTTOM: London Road Methodist Church youth club in the late 1950s. Among those in the choir are Maureen Savage, Barbara Savage, Doreen White, Margaret Proctor, Brenda Neale, Jennifer Hudson and Delphine Fenn. At the piano is Ann Sillis.

BOTTOM: Church Street in the early 1960s.
Further down the street, towards Stonegate Street, Mann Egerton have built a new garage to replace the building in the top picture.

This was subsequently demolished to form a car park although the buildings (behind the BP sign) on the corner of this street and Stonegate Street still stand.

ABOVE: Church Street in 1959. At this time Johnson's had just been purchased by Mann Egerton.

LEFT: A cutting from the Lynn News, looking North toward St James Street, shows further demolition in Church Street in 1960.

28

TOP: High Street in 1959. Looking north from the Saturday Market Place. The shop on the right in the picture is GM Hartley (ladies, children's & general drapers) and just beyond is the Cheshire Cheese pub. There was a passage between these two properties which led to Law's Yard - subject to the slum clearance of the 1930s (see *'King's Lynn in the 1930s'*).
On the left is London Central Meat and Barnard's (florists).

ABOVE: High Street in 1959. Looking in the opposite direction towards the Saturday Market Place. On the left hand side of the street can be seen the HMV and KB signs of Easters (radio, television & records) and just beyond, the Cheshire Cheese pub.
Gordon R Laidlow on the right were furniture dealers.

The King Edward VII School long photo of 1973.
Starting with the left-hand end at the top of this page and finishing with the right-hand end at the bottom of the next page.

31

TOP: St Margaret's Church Choir in 1957. The choirmaster (& organist) Victor Barker is on the left and the Reverend Aitken (who lived in the vicarage opposite the church in St Margaret's Place) is on the extreme right.
BOTTOM: St Margaret's bell ringers in 1958.
From left to right: Jill Bridges, Beryl Gibson, John 'Fred' Towler, Wendy Twite, Janice Catleugh.

ABOVE: Alderman Girls School - A gymnastics display by 3rd & 4th year girls in July 1960.
Left hand pyramid: Caroline Reed, Jane Clowser, June Lemon. *The middle (top to bottom):* Pamela Bell, Gillian Manning, ?Harrowing, Heather Barnes, Pamela Vinson, Gillian?. *Right hand pyramid:* Rita Franklin, ?, Bronka Konoska.

BOTTOM: Gaywood Park Girls 1959, Class 4 Alpha.
Back row (left to right): Jean Delaney, Linda Brock, Andrea Pottle, Jeanette Akers, Sandra Fysh, Jenny Auker.
Third row: Valerie Boar, Pamela Dunkling, Diane Reed, Pauline Kenny, Christine Overson, Betty Kent, Christine Short, Geraldine Knowles, Wendy Hall.
Second row: Jenny Birdseye, Linda High, Bernice Louro, Janet Bush, Judith Ryan, Susan Woodhouse, Christine Bolton, Avril Walker, Doreen Belcher, Pat Lucas.
Front row: Daphne Whiting, Mary Hardy, Marie Whitting, Beryl Starling, Miss Gittens, Kathleen Ross, Frederica Fulcher, Diane Jones, Janet Woodward.

ABOVE: St Margaret's Boys win the King's Lynn Schools Athletic Association shield for Primary schools in 1955.

BOTTOM: St James Girls school orchestra in 1962.
Front row (left to right): Julie Parker, Sheila Goodings, Margaret James, Jane Bright, Anne Woodward, Anne Rigby, Fiona Campbell, Linda Moyes, Daphne Riddlestone.
Back row: Includes Rosalie Harrison, Susan Hones, Linda Bennett, Jane High.

TOP: The junction of Austin Street (camera position), Blackfriars Road (opposite), Norfolk Street (to the right) and Littleport Street (to the left) in 1959. The shop on the right is Scaifes (house furnishers). The shop on the opposite corner is Mrs Tyers (greengrocer). The school sign to the left of the woman with the pram, crossing the road, is for St James Girls further along.

ABOVE: Kirby Street (off Norfolk Street) is just round the corner from Scaifes. Geoff's Taxis is at 65 Norfolk Street while Trixies (wool store) is at 67. The hoarding shows that Colin Jackson is standing as a Labour candidate and Omo adds brightness.

LEFT: A cutting from the Lynn News 1971. Kirby Street is soon to be demolished along with other nearby streets: Marshall Street, Bedford Street and Stanley Street. More of our town disappears!

THE KIRBY STREET some is typical of much 19th century building and is repeated in many parts of the country. And as in Lynn streets like this are being obliterated everywhere. (KC 9790).

ABOVE: On Saturday 12th September 1953 a South African touring side played against a Norfolk representative side. This pre-match photo was taken with Tennyson Road in the background. The gate on this day was over 6000.
BELOW LEFT: A training session on the Walks (the Baths in the background) supervised by team trainer Albert 'Bezik' Knights.
BELOW RIGHT: Albert Knights was also the team 'physio' - here he is treating forward Ray Dixon watched by manager Len Richley. 1956/58

BELOW: Lynn was not immune to the hooligan element - in 1973 when the team played Wimbledon in a FA cup game the police made several arrests. Lynn won 1-0 to advance to the next round.

ABOVE LEFT & RIGHT: The Sunday Express produced photo cards of teams in order to advertise the paper. These would be given away to fans.

ABOVE: Wisbech Road in 1968. The café on the right was owned by Fred Hendry (it had previously been run by Mrs Alexander). Across the other side of the rear access passage was Mayes Bargains, Celia's (ladies hairdressers), Tuck's (fried fish shop) and Fred Hendry (electrician).

RIGHT: Harry's News Agency in the mid - late 1960s. This was at 10, Wisbech Road.

BOTTOM: South Everard Street in November 1960. Next to Eastwoods (builders merchants) can be seen the rear access to the Bowling Green Inn which was at 68/70 Checker Street.

TOP: South Lynn station photographed from the road over-bridge shortly after closure on 28th February 1959. Now deserted - no more to reverberate to the summer sound of full trains of happy holidaymakers from the Midlands on their way to the Norfolk coast.

MIDDLE: A freight engine with a very short train crosses the Ouse from West Lynn to South Lynn. There was a speed limit of 10 mph for all trains crossing the bridge.

BELOW: A cutting from the Lynn News showing the dismantling of the bridge in October 1959. No time was lost in ripping up the line after it closed.

ABOVE: The driver of the push-pull to King's Lynn waits for an afternoon connection from a Peterborough train, due in shortly, in the mid 1950s.
The wagons on the left of the picture are on the branch from the station to the British Sugar Corporation factory.

ABOVE: The railway station in 1959 with the parcels and left luggage office to the left of the main entrance. The station took about 18 months to build and opened in October 1846 when the line to Downham and the line to Narborough opened.

MIDDLE LEFT: The telegraph office in the early 1960s. The office was on the St John's Walk side of the station near the WH Smith book stall.
MIDDLE RIGHT: Platform staff and a lady with her luggage await the arrival of the London train in the early 1960s.

BOTTOM LEFT: 1959. By the late 1950s diesel locomotives were becoming a common sight.
A class 31 diesel waits to depart with a train to (ultimately) Liverpool Street, while a class D16 steam locomotive (built in 1911 and in it's last few months of service before scrapping) waits to depart for Hunstanton.
BOTTOM RIGHT: Ernie Anderson receives driving instruction from Louis Manning-Coe in the cab of a new diesel multiple unit (DMU). These two car units replaced steam hauled trains from 1955 onwards (initially on the Dereham line) and would cut running costs but this still didn't stop line closures later in the 1960s.

TOP: An unknown class of Alderman Catleugh Girls in 1959 with Mrs Bell.

ABOVE: Gaywood Park Girls class 3B in 1961.
Back row (left to right): Christine Ruhms, Eileen Foster, Diane Dexter, Pauline Hammond, Pat Lee, Eileen Merrikin, Avril Oakes, Sandra Setchell, Yvonne Harrod.
Third row: Ann Paddy, Thelma Church, Sandra Scase, Teresa Eke, Sandra Dennis, Pat Lockley, Anne Borrmann.
Second row: Henrietta Mendham, Sandra Trigwell, Susan Gordon, Pamela Kirby, ?, Janet?, Jennifer Moyes, Christine Girdlestone, June Pratt.
Front row: Helen Maine, Maureen Webb, ?, Virginia Pidgeon, Mrs Sullivan, Carol Hipkin, Doreen Jenkinson, Susan High, Linda Holman?.

ABOVE: All Saints Christmas Party in 1961.
Front row (left to right): Julie Mierhofer, Carole Scott, Doreen Willingham, Carol Knight, Joan Barker, Linda Cooper, Angela Mason, Susan Hodgson.
Back row: Olive Murray, ?, Anna Kaligna, Mary Loasby, Susan Smith, Angela Thrower, Janine Rose, Heather McKenzie.

LEFT: 1952. Winners of a swimming gala at The Walks Swimming Pool (The Baths)

BELOW LEFT: 1963. High School open day. A record request show.

BELOW RIGHT: Gaywood Park Girls School in 1961. French teacher Mrs Griggs with some of her students.

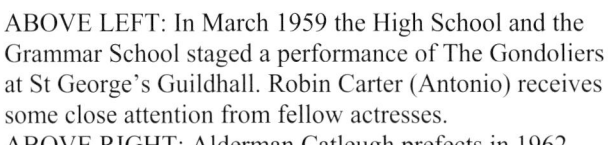

ABOVE LEFT: In March 1959 the High School and the Grammar School staged a performance of The Gondoliers at St George's Guildhall. Robin Carter (Antonio) receives some close attention from fellow actresses.
ABOVE RIGHT: Alderman Catleugh prefects in 1962.
Back row (left to right): June Roberts, Nannette Lock, Janet Chilvers, Susan Bretten, Lynda Brett, Janet Boon, Ann Frankham.
Front row (left to right): Fiona Lawson, Maureen Rudd, Sue Mansell (head girl), Sheila Riddlestone, Carole Stimpson.

TOP LEFT: St Nicholas Street looking east towards the junction of Chapel Street and St Ann's Street in May 1961. The shop signs on the right belong to PT Bowdich (shopkeeper), and beyond is the Duke of Connaught and St Nicholas Drill Hall.
TOP RIGHT: A view in the opposite direction, looking towards the Tuesday Market Place, in 1959. The Victory Inn is on the corner - it closed two years later in March 1961. Today, 50 years later, St Nicholas Street is extremely busy.
BOTTOM: Looking down St Ann's Street from St Ann's Fort in the early 1960s.

Bob's doing well now bridge is re-opened

ABOVE LEFT: Haynes Garage at the bottom of Dodman's Bridge in the early 1960s.

ABOVE RIGHT: In 1970 there was disruption on Gaywood Road owing to repairs on the bridge. The garage owner, Bob Gladding, was so pleased to get back to normal that he offered a discount on petrol, oil and tyres!

LEFT: May 1961. A steady stream of cars leave town down Littleport Street, and beyond, Norfolk Street.

BOTTOM: January 1963 – the coldest winter on record. Looking east along Littleport Street, the re-assuring sight of a lone 'bobby' on his way to his Gaywood beat.
Lynn Service Station can be seen on the right.

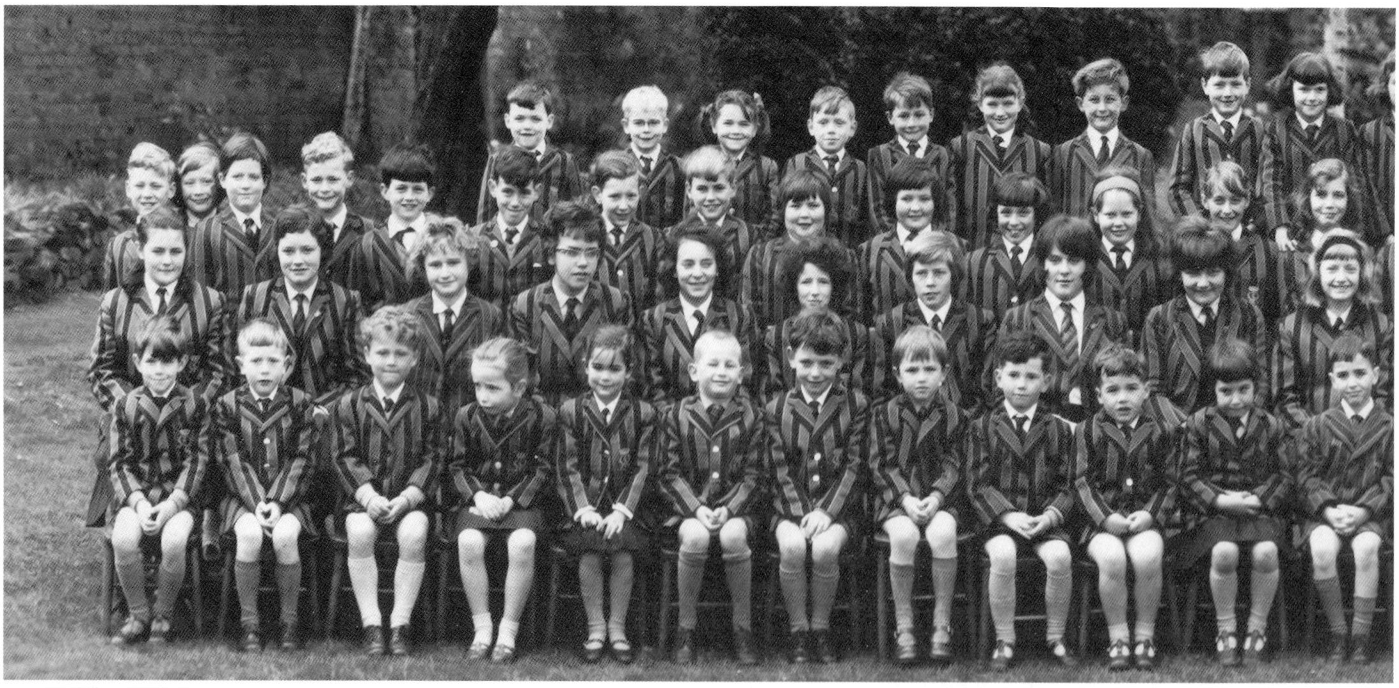

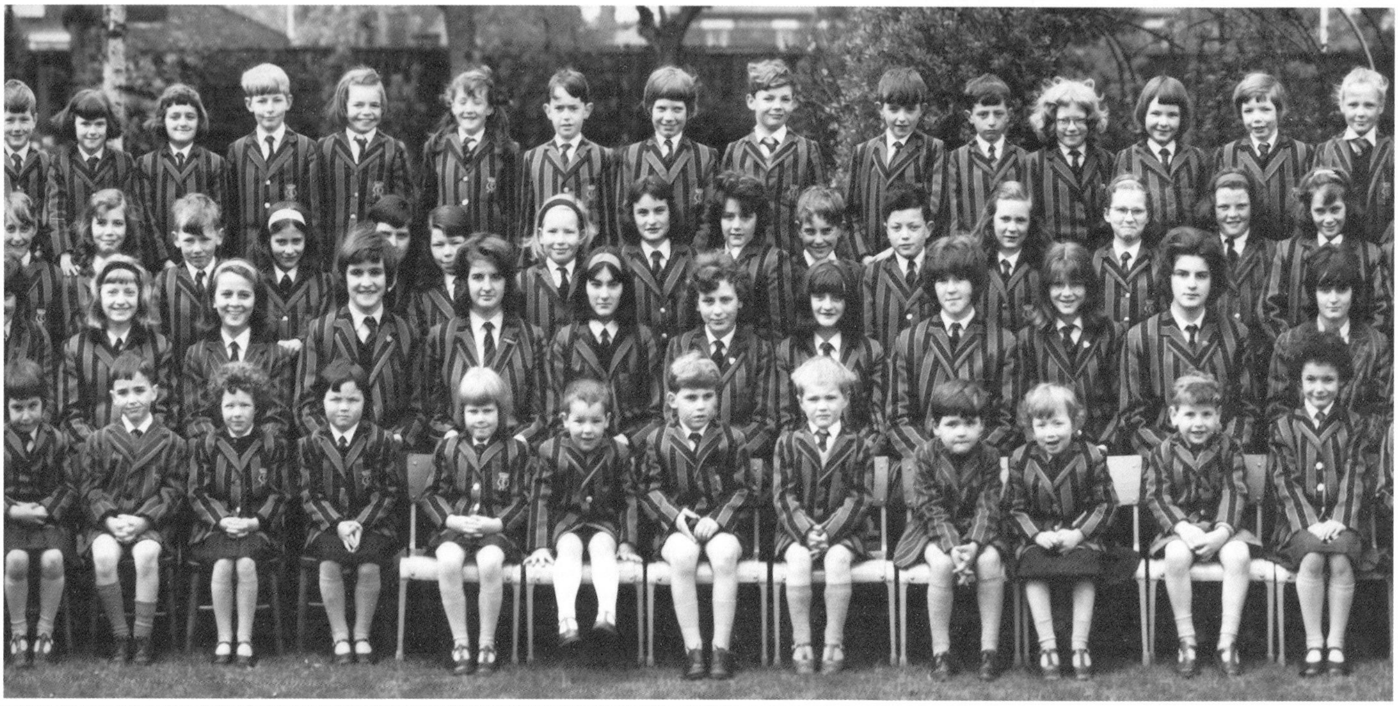

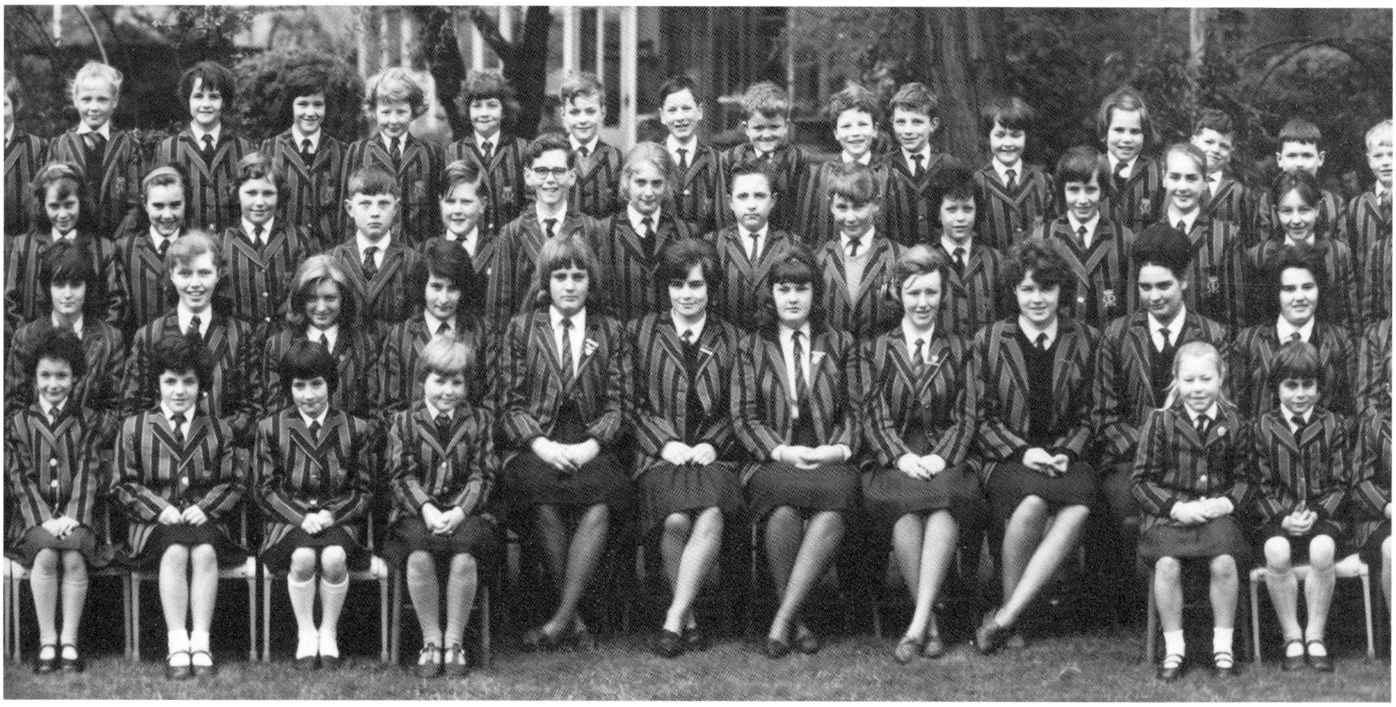

Opposite page and above: The long photo of The Convent in 1960.

The Servite Convent (high school for girls and preparatory school for girls and boys) was at 39 & 41 Goodwin's Road.

RIGHT: 29th April 1963.
The Convent on a trip to London.
Here the girls are feeding the pigeons in Trafalgar Square.

The trip also included a visit to Hampton Court and to see 'The Sound of Music'.

45

LEFT: The 6th West Lynn Brownies in 1962. The Brown Owl was Mrs Smalley and the Tawny Owl was Janice Catleugh.

They met at West Lynn St Peters Parish church rooms.

Back row (left to right): Linda Self, Jane Sheard, Yvonne Smalley, Mary Barrett, Sally Fulford, Benita Curry.
Middle row: Anne Woodward, Dulcie Sawford, Christine Dodman, Jenny Scott, Linda Cressingham, Janice Smith, Lyn White.
Front row: Gillian Griffiths, Lynne Howlett, ?, Deborah Haylock, Ann Fountain, Roslyn Hare.

ABOVE: 1957. Gaywood Park Class 2 Beta.
Back row (left to right): Dulcia Temby, Victoria Weldrick, Sandra Pepper, Freda Artis, Margaret Eke, Pamela Childerhouse, Rosemary Page, Elaine Stokes, Wendy Oakes, Juliet Hornigold.
Third row: Maxine Clark, Barbara Girdlestone, Jennifer Adams, Pamela Warnes, Kathleen Roper, Pamela Mendham, Pearl Lee, Shirley Bunn, Pat Bone, Judith Folker.
Second row: Iris Chilvers, Daphne Bilham, Janis Curtis, Janet Pointer, Christine Perry, Lucille Garnett, Patricia Bodsworth, Janet Fowel, Sylvia Young, Sheila McGregor.
Front row: Elizabeth Chase, Daphne Ess, Jacqueline Ding, Brenda Evetts, Carole Twiddy, Mary Veal, Eileen Rowel, Jane Harper, Barbara Jackson, Jean Large.

TOP: 1963. Campbell's staff ready for the outing to the London Palladium to see Harry Secombe.

ABOVE: 1965. All Saint's school trip ready to go to Springfields (Spalding) and Crowland Abbey. Teachers accompanying the group are Miss Ward, Miss Baldry and Mrs Bonham (headmistress). All Saints' Primary Girls and Primary Infants School was in South Everard Street. The infant school was built in 1852 and the girl's primary class rooms were added in 1899.

SCOTT & SON
(KING'S LYNN) LTD.

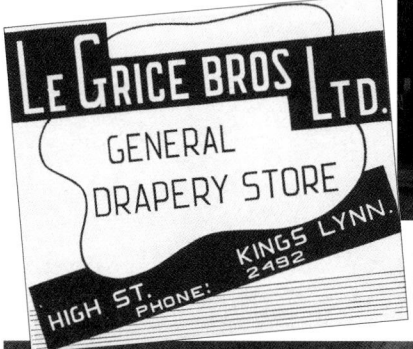

Complete House Furnishers

DEPARTMENTS:
FURNITURE, FLOOR COVERINGS,
BEDDING, GLASSWARE AND CHINA,
DRAPERY, HARDWARE, TOYS,
NURSERY FURNITURE, PRAMS

SCOTT & SON ARE MANUFACTURERS OF
FURNITURE AND BEDDING

WRITE, PHONE OR CALL AT:
91-97 HIGH ST. – 1-3 PURFLEET ST.
KING'S LYNN

ESTABLISHED 1874   TELEPHONE 2495

LE GRICE BROS LTD.
GENERAL DRAPERY STORE
HIGH ST. PHONE: 2492 KINGS LYNN

ABOVE: High Street in 1960, looking towards the Tuesday Market Place on an August afternoon. High Street is the second longest shopping street in Lynn (about ½ mile in length). The mid-summer sales are still on. *A £1 note in 1960 would be worth about £16 today.*

ABOVE: Late in November 1962. High Street is still busy although it's near closing time. No late night or Sunday shopping, the town shops worked a 5½ day week, and were always well staffed to give good service and most made a profit. Nowadays staff are spread so thinly that there is usually no time to properly attend to customers needs - often resulting in lost sales.

The Stanley library had been founded in 1854 by Lord Stanley. It was installed in The Athenaeum* in Blackfriars Street. In 1884, on being given notice to quit the Athenaeum, a new library was built in St James Road (opposite the St James Park). This was named 'The Stanley Building'. Then in May 1905 the current Carnegie (or Free) Library was opened.

* The Athenaeum became the GPO - until it was recently closed.

LEFT: In the early 1950s Barbara Fall serves Patricia, who is the 6th millionth borrower, watched by borough librarian Mr CH Senior.

BELOW: Staff mark the 50th anniversary of opening by releasing tagged balloons - a prize being given for the one found farthest away - although five went no further than the Millfleet!. The staff from the left: Miss E Booth, Barbara Fall, Mrs Jill Smith, Miss D Asker, Mr Senior, Miss G Hanton, Mrs M Hart, Miss J Bowden, Mrs D Human.

ABOVE: Marks and Spencer Christmas party at the Dukes Head in 1965. 'Marks & Spencer's Hoppers' do the Charleston.
Left to right: Joyce Foster, Peggy Anderson, Barbara Fendley, Mina Mott, Gwen Curston, Miss Youngs, Elsie Barker, Heather Rix, Irene Wilkinson, Gladys Fendley.

ABOVE: Christmas 1958. A New Year's conga spills out of the Dukes Head into the Tuesday Market Place.
Probably the first time the dance has been done by someone wearing a coat and scarf and smoking a pipe at the same time!

TOP: A view from Campbell's siding to Hardwick Road in July 1959. The siding joined the London line at Harbour Junction.
MIDDLE: An aerial view of the early development of the Hardwick Industrial Estate in the early 1960s. Campbell's factory and tower is clearly visible - although for not much longer as the site has been bought by a supermarket who intend to demolish it.
BOTTOM LEFT & RIGHT: Hardwick Road in 1968.
Compared with a few years earlier (see *'Another Look Back at Lynn'* - page 15) traffic has certainly increased considerably.

Norfolk Street 1950

1 Brice Miss Lilian, Confectioner
2 Middletons (Frucon) Ltd. Fruiterers
2a, Dewhurst JH Ltd Butchers
3
4 Ely Wm. & Sons Bakers
5 Metcalf & Spreckley Ltd Chemists

here is White Lion Court

6
7/8 Plowright Pratt & Harbage, Ironmongers
9 Singer Sewing Machine Co Ltd
10 Kay's Stores, Grocers
11 Fiddamans Hotel (Nicholls & Campbell) Ltd
12 Nicholls & Campbell Ltd
13 Grosvenor Restaurant

here is Broad Street

14 Catleughs of Lynn Ltd. Outfitters
15/16 Lock William & Son Ltd (contractors)
17 Lock Chas B, Butcher
18 Brighter Home Stores, Wallpaper merchants
19 Bird-in-Hand PH
19/20 Davy Bros, Drapers
21 Crown Wallpapers Ltd
22/24 Kirklands Tailors
25 Twite Albert Grocer
26 Keal CH Butcher
27 Culey JW Fruiterer
28 Miller Reg Fried fish shop
29 Giles ER & Son Ltd. Heating engineers
30 Barnard Mrs. Tobacconist
30a, Wharton Ernest, Boot repairer
31 Giles ER & Son Ltd. Electrical engineers

here is Paradise Lane

32 Harrison & Wilson, Saddlers
33
34 Pank Alfd. Printer
35 Doranne, Baby linen warehouse
36 Edmunds Thos W Hardware dealer
36a Cresswell & Thompsett, Motor body repairs
37 Riches Stanley, Fishmonger
38 Riches Wm C Tool merchant
40 Warrington Percy, Tobacconist
41 Sheldrake Regnld Greengrocer
42 Easter Mrs M Confectioner
43 Stapletons Dairies Ltd. Ice cream manufacturers
44 Marsters Frank, Boot & shoe dealer
45 Townsend Charles Ltd. Corn merchants

here is Railway Road

49 Barber Charles A Family butcher
50 Waters Mrs Ada Confectioner
51 Barber Chas A Butcher (store)
52 East Miss A Confectioner
53 Higgleton Mrs A M Newsagent & tobacconist
54 Turner Arth C
55 Morris Fredk R
56 Morley Herbt Pork butcher
57 Ash Chas Fredk Tobacconist
58/59
60 Koziel Marian
61 Frost Geo. Edwd. Greengrocer
62 Thurston Ernest E. Boot repairer
64 Mason Wilfred F Butcher

here is Kirby Street

65 Suckling Edwd. Butcher
66 Green Mrs. B
67 Warren Stanley B. Confectioner
68 Large Ernest, Hairdresser
69 Gray Jn R Cycle agent
70 Bracher Fredk
70a, Clements Mrs. H. Shopkeeper
70b, Arminger Dawson, Fruiterer

Norfolk Street 1975

1 Kandi Kabin, confectioners
1a Lynn Travel, travel agents
2a, Dewhurst JH Ltd. Butchers
3 Coffee House, Restaurant
4 Halfords Ltd, cycle agents
5 Clyde 3, men's boutique

here is White Lion Court

6 Sketchley Ltd, dry cleaners
7/8
9 Singer Sewing Machine Co Ltd
10/11
12 Eastern Electricity
13 Provincial Building Society
14 Carter FS, TV, Electrical, Radio

here is Broad Street

15 Catleughs of Lynn Ltd. Outfitters
16 Lynn Carpet Centre Ltd. Carpet retailers
17 Lock G & Son, Butchers
18 Matthes Ltd. Bakers
19 Bird-in-Hand PH
20
21 Crown Wallpapers
22/24 Kirklands Tailors & outfitters
25 Lynn Carpet Centre
26 Stanfords, Fruiterers
27 Rix BD Television engineer
28 Miller Regnld. Fried fish shop
29 Chilvers LJ Ltd Fancy goods dealers
30 Sewing Machine Centre
30a Baby Boutique, Childrens outfitters
31

here is Paradise Lane

32
33 Rowlinson's Sports & Toys Ltd.
34
35
36 Lynnlec Ltd Domestic electrical appliances
36a King's Lynn Glass &Trimming Co
37 Riches Stanley, Fishmonger
38 Chilvers A Tool merchant
40 Hall WA & Co. Chemists
41 Solesta Costumiers
42 Kershaw L & J Confectioners
43 Eric's Discount Stores Ironmongers
44 Percy's Pride, tape and record shop
45 Wheelers, Stork Corner, Baby carriage dealers

here is Railway Road

49 Suzettes Flowers, Florists
50 Miss Linda Hair Fashions
51 Parker R. Watchmaker
52 Yates Kenneth G
53 Back Mrs Al. Newsagent
54 Turner Raymond A
55
56 Blackfriars School of Motoring
57
58/59 Bellbrae Ltd., builders
60 Young Ones, Ladies' hairdressers
61 Tyler B. grocer
62 Lynn Discery, record dealers
63/64 Mason Wilfred F Butcher

here is Kirby Street

65 Bronte, Gowns
66 Bronte, Gowns
67 Twinette, ladies hairdressers
68
69 Plumb & Farmer (Heating) Ltd, heating & plumbing
70 Houchen Cumbley, antique dealer
70a Norfolk Investigation Agency
70b

These two pages compare the occupancy of shops over the 25 years covered by this book. Gaps usually mean that the shop is currently empty. Norfolk Street is the longest shopping street in town - approximately ⅔ of a mile.

here is Blackfriars Road	**here is Blackfriars Road**
71 Sizeland Edwd	71
72	72
73 Burrell Mrs. D	73
74 Earl Edwd. Jn	74
75 Limbert's Ltd. Fried fish shop	76 Anglian Carpet Services
77	77 Anglian Carpet Services.
78 Bradfield Ibberson & Co. Ltd. Warehouseman	78 Bradfield Ibberson & Co. Ltd.
79 Bennett RS & Co. Ltd. Agricultural engineers	79 Bennett RS & Co. Ltd. Agricultural engineers
80 Senter Mrs	
82 Carman Jn	
84/90 King's Lynn Co-operative Society Ltd	84/90 King's Lynn Co-operative Society Ltd
here is Railway Passage	**here is John Kennedy Road**
92 Andrews Mrs IM Chemist	95 Modern Boot Repairing Co
93 Long Mrs Gladys M Hardware	96 Rice David & Partners, estate agents
94 East Kenneth H & Co. Rope manufacturers	97 Spaxman, Fruiterer
95 Modern Boot Repairing Co	97a Brien Harry, French polisher & Taylor, upholsterer
96 Turner Geo Wm Tobacconist & post office	98 Hat Box Milliners & costume jewellery
97 Spaxman Cyril Wm. Florist	99 Work Box haberdashery, wool, trimming
98 Charles Valentine Ltd. Wine & spirits	100 Barnes Maurice & Son Leather & boot merchant
99 Smith Bros. Army Stores, Clothiers	101 Dewhurst, China dealers
100 Barnes Maurice & Son, Wholesale leather merchants	102 Dressrite, dressmaker
101 Bargate China Co. China dealers	103 Scupham Chas W & Son, Pork butchers
102	104 Rowlinsons Sports & Toys
103 Scupham Chas W & Son, Pork butchers	105 Thomas Mark Geo. Butcher
104 Norwich Arms P.H.	106
105 Thomas Mark Geo. Butcher	107 Taylor DR, upholsterers, soft furnishers & linens
106 King's Lynn & District Working Men's Co-op. Soc. Butchers	108 Van Pelt Mrs F Pork butcher
107 Towler Jn Chas. Hairdresser	109 Limberts Ltd. Restaurant
108	110 Eagle Hotel
	112 Fine Fare, Grocers
Demolished after bombing in 1942	113 Fine Fare, Grocers
	114 Fine Fare, Grocers
114 Steward-Brown FM Draper	
here is Albert Street	**here is Albert Street**
115 Hayes JB & Son, chemists	115 Ingrams (Boston) Ltd. Seedsmen
116 Ebling Frank, Fancy goods dealer	116 Do it Yourself Centre
117 Bray E newsagent & Stationer	117 Wilson R Newsagent
118	118
119 Reynolds (Norfolk) Ltd. Bakers	119 Wagg TR (The Baker) Ltd
120 Gazley G H (Chester B. Pegg) Outfitter	120 Gazley (King's Lynn) Ltd. Outfitters
121 Pearks Dairies Ltd. Provision dealers	121 Wimpy Bar, Café
122 Holman & Fawcett Ltd. China dealers	122 Parish Bros (Norwich) Ltd., carpet retailers
123 Melias Ltd. Grocers	123 Stratfords Ltd (Army Stores), Clothiers
124 Army & Navy Stores (Stratfords Ltd) Clothiers	124 Stratfords Ltd (Army Stores), Clothiers
125 Baxter Mrs. Alice E. Greengrocer	125 Scotts China Shop,
126 Hulme Bros Butchers	126 Donaldson Andrew Ltd, Fishmongers
127 Culey Jn T Corn merchant	127 Culey RE pet foods
127a Oswell Geo R & Son Printers	127a Harry's Warehouse, Antique dealers
128 Langford & Fidment Tobacconists	128
129 Langford Emerson, Ironmonger	129
130 Wilson H & J Ltd. Costumiers	130
131 Wilson H & J Ltd. Costumiers	131
132 Flower Pot PH	132 Downsway, supermarket
here is Chapel Street	**here is Chapel Street**
133 Chain Libraries Ltd. Lending library	133
134 Turner Fredk. Rt. Hairdresser	134 Turners, ladies hairdressers
135 Hirst Wm. Stanley, Jeweller	135 Wain F Jeweller
136 London Central Meat Co. Ltd. Butchers	136 Baxters (Butchers) Ltd
137 Sadler Mrs EH Costumier	137 Hardy & Co House furnishers
138 Winton-Smith F. Ltd. Cooked meats	138 Hardy & Co House furnishers
139 Forum Cleaners & Dyers Ltd	139
140 Brooke Ht. Jn. China dealer	140 Barrons (King's Lynn) Ltd. Outfitters
141 Donaldson's, Fishmongers	141
142 Taylor R & A Seed & bulb merchants	142 Taylor R & A Ltd. Seedsmen
143 Millett EG & Co Ltd Clothiers	143 Millett AC & Co Ltd Clothiers
144	144
145 Mann Egerton & Co Ltd Motor agents & dealers	145 Marks & Spencer Ltd. Departmental stores
146 Marks & Spencer Ltd. Bazaar	146 Marks & Spencer Ltd. Departmental stores

There are a few unexplained discrepancies in the numbering. Over the years White Lion Court is listed between 4 & 5, 6 & 7 Norfolk Street but I believe it should be between 5 & 6 Norfolk Street.
During the late 1960s/early 1970s rebuilding, the address of 14 Norfolk Street (Catleughs) jumps across Broad Street to become FS Carter.

LEFT: 1970. A 'Tec' class of new students pose for the camera at the beginning of their course. Students came from a large area of Norfolk to usually take a two year 'O' level course. Some carried on to take 'A' levels or higher qualifications before leaving.

RIGHT: Gaywood Park Girls in June 1972.

Back row: Kim Smith, Angela Hooks, Linda Skipper, Julie Bunting, Jane English, Shirley McLellan, Julie Hurn.
Third row: Lorrie Younger, Karen Miller, Amanda Jane Smith, Karen Tarbuck, Susan Gamble, Brenda Howlett, Sharon Rankin.
Second row: Stephanie Donger, Shanie Williamson, Lynn Barnard, Janet O'Conner, Teresa Crome, Linda Judd, Bridget Panks, Jeannie Panks, Verena Mayes.
Front row: Julie Bone, Pat Branham, Julie Clarke, Linda Setchell, Mrs Hoadley, Linda Eagle, Debra Fisher, Linda Greff, Ann McKensey.

BOTTOM: Class 2B Gaywood Park Boys in 1957. The teacher is Mr Bayes - no connection to the well-known record shop of the same name!

TOP: The Pelicans Hockey teams in 1965.
Back row (left to right): G Baxter, I Neave, B Thompson, D Wroth, M Heading, P Cole, K Crawford, J Carter, M Boon, J Oliver.
Middle row: R Everett, R Rose, J Rose, M Cox, L Driver, W Landles, J Cross, C Robbins, D Horn, J Sharpe, P Dealtrey, P Andrews, B Jakes.
Front row: R Atkins, A Burman, M Vauser, J Mapus-Smith, J Palmer, J Wroth, G Thomas, N Carter, A Brett, D Whitmore, W Gemmell, R Pugh.

ABOVE LEFT: King's Lynn Hockey club 1958/59. *Back row:* J Neep, B Hilton, D Oliver, G Payne, A Haigh, J Lupson.
Front row: T Braddock, B Batterham, Mr Brown, B Belton, John Bell, ?, M Woods.
ABOVE RIGHT: West Norfolk Fertilisers football team 1963/64. Borough Cup, League Cup & Norfolk Junior Cup winners.
Back row: Bobby Steward, Alec Willgress, Ted Wilkerson, Eric Bingley, Tony Ward, Ivan Hall, David Farrow, Charlie Farrow, Sonny Sands.
Front row: Brian Gibbs, Jimmy Steward, Doug Human, Jimmy Anderson, Gerald Groom.

RIGHT: Gaywood Park Boys Under 13, 1960.

Back row (left to right): Kenny Bloom, Mick Sayer, Peter Holland, John Catton, Chris Taylor, Kevin Fickling.

Front row: Bob Mann, Michael Hodgson Trevor Howard*, Eric Trigg, Tony Hemeter, Martin Bloom.

*Trevor Howard went on to play for Norwich City.

TOP: Townsend's Corner in the early 1960s, looking east. The imposing frontage of 'The King's Lynn & District Co-Operative Society Limited' can clearly be seen. Opposite, on the corner, is aptly named 'Flower Corner'.
BOTTOM: By the mid 1970s Fenland Insurance (fronting both Railway Road and Norfolk Street). This was originally Charles Townsend (corn merchant). On the extreme left of the photo a car is just exiting Oldsunway.

OPPOSITE PAGE TOP: By 1965 part of Norfolk Street had been demolished to make way for the John Kennedy Road. The breakthrough had been achieved by November 1963.
OPPOSITE PAGE BOTTOM: An aerial view in 1963, showing the progress being made on the link road (bottom middle of picture) from Railway Road to the docks.

57

ABOVE: A summer's day in St James Street 1961. The last three shops along the street in the left: William Crome (decorator), Woods (newsagents) and Bayes TV Ltd. Beyond is the Police Station. The facing building on London Road is St James' Methodist Chapel.

BOTTOM: Further down St James Street, looking in the same direction but the year before, 1960. Businesses on the left are: Wards Fruit Stores, Auto School of Motoring, Bears Corn Stores and Wheelers (radio dealers). Beyond the top of Tower Street is the Rummer Hotel (postal address - Tower Street). The businesses on the right of the picture are FW Bennell (bakers), AG Sawyer (butcher), WH Johnson (motor engineers).

King Edward VII School

TOP LEFT: The combined cadet force - there were the army cadets and the RAF cadets. An inspecting officer questions student Colin Johnson, watched by member of staff, Mr (Flying Officer) Gregory.
The school had a glider but unfortunately, in 1958, an over enthusiastic student crashed it on the school field!
TOP RIGHT: This photo (1955) has a caption *'officer training course'?*

MIDDLE LEFT: Open day at KES, a cadet tries to impress the girls with his 'not-so-mobile' phone.
MIDDLE RIGHT: There were two orders of punishment (if the cane is not included) -punishment parade after school or detention on a Saturday afternoon - the school operated on Saturday morning - a 5½ week. Here the headmaster oversees a typical punishment parade - rolling his beloved cricket square.
Not so easy when only a few are on that day's parade.
LOWER MIDDLE RIGHT: A group of 5th formers pose for the camera man - outside the lavatories!

BOTTOM RIGHT: It appears that the very strict regime we had endured in the 1960s and before was beginning to be relaxed when, in 1971, the school had a rag week.
Here masters (being transported, of course) are pushed by students in a wheelbarrow race - Mr Middleton in the lead!

59

TOP Scouts from the Lynn area at a 1968 jamboree at Sennowe Park near Fakenham.
BELOW RIGHT: King's Lynn 7th Scout troop in 1964 at the Guildhall with Ralph Reader (of London Gang Show fame).
Left to right: David Underwood, Bernard McLean, John Webber, Peter Godfrey, Ralph Reader, Johnny Morris (hidden), Pat Heaphy and Bob Fisher.

ABOVE:
On 29th October 1963 members of 42(F) Lynn Training Corps Squadron welcome the mayor, Alderman Albert Bacon to the Majestic for the first showing of 'The Great Escape'.

RIGHT: In October 1963 the new centre for Lynn St. Raphael Club is opened by Mrs Iain McLeod, wife of the leader of the House of Commons.
Also present is Viscount Althorp (president of the club) and Mr Goldsworthy (Goldy) - in striped shirt.

TOP: 1965. A view of Stevens Corner (the junction of Railway Road, Blackfriars Street, St James' Road and St John's Terrace. The shop had been occupied by Carters (electric domestic appliances, TV &radio) and within the next year would become Geoffrey Collings (estate agents) and King's Lynn Building Society.

ABOVE: A view looking south up Railway Road to Stevens Corner on a Spring afternoon in 1963. On the right of the picture a Thorne's van is delivering confectionery to Leslie C Watson's (wholesale confectionery) at their Imperial Rooms depot. The Imperial Rooms were part of what was originally 'The Tabernacle'. This had been built in 1853 by the Wesleyan Reform Association or Methodist New Connexion. The rest of the building was used by BW Johnson (plumber, painter & decorator) in 1963.

LEFT: The Tabernacle Imperial Rooms (on the left of the picture) just before demolition in 1981. The right-hand part of the Tabernacle still remains today although with a much altered façade from the original.

TOP: The Walks - Toni Byrne and Jenny Sorella show off the first trouser suits in Lynn in 1964.

MIDDLE LEFT: 1966. Toni Byrne dared Tony Lidgard to walk down Norfolk Street in a miniskirt she had made. He appeared again at a fashion show at the Town Hall - for a fund raising evening to raise money for the Aberfan disaster.

MIDDLE RIGHT: My uncle (Bill Booth) drew a cartoon for the Lynn News showing what might happen if the idea caught on!

RIGHT: Lynn News reporter Dick Taylor interviews some Tec students on issues of the day for his 'Young Set' page.

In 1958 Tec students had been barred from a 'popular coffee bar haunt'. They were told by college staff to stay away because of the 'teds'. "*One master said we would end up in Borstal if we mixed with them*" said one student.

Broad Street

TOP LEFT & RIGHT: On a cold, snowy 5th December 1962. A corner of the Cattle Market - the hoardings show there's bingo on at the Theatre Royal and another proclaims '*Dear Santa we want a new tele for Xmas*'. Reed's (newsagents) and Anglia Restaurant can be seen. The winter of 1962/63 was the coldest for over 200 years.

MIDDLE: Looking south down the street towards the Post Office in February 1965.

BOTTOM LEFT: 1965. The Cattle Market Tavern and N Mayes (second-hand dealer) are either side of Baptist's Yard*.

BOTTOM RIGHT: 1965. Looking north to Norfolk Street.

* Photos of Baptist's Yard can be seen in '*King's Lynn in the 1930s*' - still currently available.

TOP: June 1966. Some of the 500 staff and families of British Industrial Sand at the ticket barrier ready to board their own 'BIS Special' train to Yarmouth. On the right is Sid Gathercole the ticket collector.
ABOVE: In 1961 Jermyn's staff pose at the front of the station before their day out.
LEFT: The magazine 'Rail News' was optimistic about the future of Lynn station in 1965. Ticket collector Bert Jacobs, who had been at Lynn since 1937 was looking forward to the increased traffic that the overspill scheme would bring. Unfortunately within five years both the Lynn - Dereham line and the Lynn - Hunstanton lines were closed thanks to Ernest Marples. Marples (Minister of Transport 1959 to 1964) had employed Dr Richard Beeching to take an axe to the railway. Marples had been a director of road construction company Marples-Ridgeway! The cost of closure was thousands of railway workers jobs. Ironically Mr Marples fled the country in 1975, never to return, due to tax irregularities.

RIGHT: 1961. Will Everard (built 1925) in the Purfleet.
This Thames sailing barge was a regular visitor between 1955 & 1966.
Her cargo of 270 tons of wheat was loaded here and delivered to Hull.

BELOW LEFT: 11th July 1962. High water where the Purfleet joins the Ouse. The tug Conservator (owned by the King's Lynn Conservancy Board) is moored on the Purfleet Hard Quay. The tug had been sold to a new owner at Blyth and would leave for the North East within the next 24 hours.

BELOW RIGHT: The (almost) same spot on Saturday 2nd February 1963. The winter of 1962/63 was the hardest winter in living memory - the stern of the Sincerity can be seen on the right of the picture.

BOTTOM: Again on 2nd February 1963 the Sincerity (owned by FT Everard) has been loaded with wheat destined for Glasgow.

The Boal Quay

TOP: The Sanguity arrives on 27th April 1960 with a cargo of 1795 tons of phosphate from Casablanca destined for the 'Muck Works'.

MIDDLE LEFT to MIDDLE RIGHT:
- The Boal Quay with a carpet of spilt phosphate, showing wagons for loading from two unidentified ships.
- The crane driver operates from above.
- The crane deposits it's load to transfer the phosphate from ship to wagon.

LEFT: A view into the hold of a 'phosphate' ship. Note the man standing in the hold. In earlier times before 'grab buckets' were used men would have to get in the hold and shovel the phosphate into 'crane buckets'. Another of the many dirty hard jobs men had to do to earn a living.

ABOVE: Shunting from the South Quay across the Millfleet using a tractor in 1963. Steam locomotives had been banned from the South Quay since 1955.

LEFT: The dredger 'Breckland' is moored on the South Quay in October 1960. She has returned from the Lynn Channel dumping silt removed from the docks

BOTTOM: September 1962. South Quay. The Atomicity (owned by FT Everard) would load 663 tons of raw sugar for London. Sold to a Greek company in 1966 and renamed the Eolos, she was sunk by a mine off Tripoli in 1973.

TOP: A view looking west down the Millfleet (or the 'Fleet') from London Road on a Sunday morning in the early 1960s.
MIDDLE: The Millfleet in 1960. It's just after 4 pm on a sunny afternoon as school children make their way home. The 38A bus waits to depart to North Lynn.
BOTTOM: Stonegate Street looking east toward the Fleet. On the corner of the Fleet and Tower Place is the Eastern Counties Omnibus Co. Ltd (booking office) again taken on the Sunday morning in the early 1960s. The building on the left of the photo belongs to RH Bolton (printers) while the taller building in the middle of the picture is the Stonegate Hotel & Restaurant.

LEFT: Between Scott & Son Ltd. (Nos. 91 - 97 High Street and Montague Burton Ltd. (Nos. 98 - 99) is Purfleet Street.

ABOVE RIGHT: A view down Purfleet Street from High Street in June 1963. By this time most of the premises on the right hand side were derelict except for Scott's (Nos. 1 - 4), Lynn News (Nos. 12 & 13) and Winloves (Nos. 14 & 15), cabinet makers.

BOTTOM: August 1960. A view looking up Purfleet Street towards New Conduit Street. The driver of the Scott's van gets last minute instruction before leaving on a delivery. Behind the van the shops on this side are: Scott's (house furnishings), Fred Dale (pork butcher) and Mrs EM Hornigold (tobacconist). The large warehouse on the right of the picture also belongs to Scott's.

ABOVE: 1966. North Lynn, Seabank estate, looking north. The square in the right bottom corner of the estate is Chadwick Square.
The Hunstanton railway line stretches out toward North Wootton Station some 2 miles away.
The Hunstanton line was closed in May 1969.
RIGHT: 1957. Prefabs in St Edmundsbury Road. These had been built at the end of the war in order to satisfy a need for short term housing demand.

BELOW: The new Chadwick Square in November 1966. Like the old prefabs, these houses were also built using modern prefabricated units in order to speed up the building programme.

Lynn News cutting: Oct' 1958.

Prefabs on the Tarran Estate at North Lynn which may shortly be dismantled, having served their useful purpose.

D-Day for Future of King's Lynn 'Pre-fabs'

TODAY is decision day for the future of King's Lynn's only "pre-fabs," the 50 Tarran bungalows on the North Lynn estate. The Borough Council is to be asked to authorise the rehousing of the occupants so that the houses can be removed

January sales in full sway

SPEEDWAY LEAGUE FOR LYNN STARS

Track thrills ahead at South Lynn

AFTER two months of speculation, Lynn Stars have been admitted to the British Speedway League for the coming season, which opens at Easter. This good news was welcomed by co-promoters Maurice Littlechild and Cyril Crane at the weekend, and will be well received by the many speedway enthusiasts in East Anglia.

It has also set the ball rolling for important developments at South Lynn Stadium where speedway was held last year for the first time. Work is expected to begin this week to provide covered accommodation along the entire length of the back straight, and later it is intended to install seating for up to 300 spectators.

As seen in the Lynn News in 1966
FROM TOP LEFT: Scott's January sales begin; a boy has to be rescued from the Greyfriars tower; All Saints Street is about to be demolished to make way for Hillington Square.
LEFT: When Norwich lost their speedway due to redevelopment in 1964, Lynn opened it's track at Saddlebow Road on 23rd May 1965.
BELOW: Members of Lynn Motor Club collect their prizes at an annual dinner.

ABOVE: Four of the prize winners at Lynn Motor Club dinner at Hunstanton Country Club on Friday are (left to right) Mr. F. H. Piggins, Mr. E. Markham, Mr. J. Brundle and Mr T. W. Cammack.

High School second stage takes shape

RIVETTS OF LYNN
51 and 77 HIGH STREET, KING

'New' Hillington Square

ABOVE LEFT: The Hardwick to Castle Rising bypass almost ready to open.

ABOVE RIGHT: The new High School is into stage two of construction off Gayton Road. This would eventually combine with the Alderman Catleugh to form Springwood High School.

LEFT: Rivetts of 51 High Street open their re-designed enlarged dress room.
RIGHT: A model of the new £1.1 million Hillington Square.

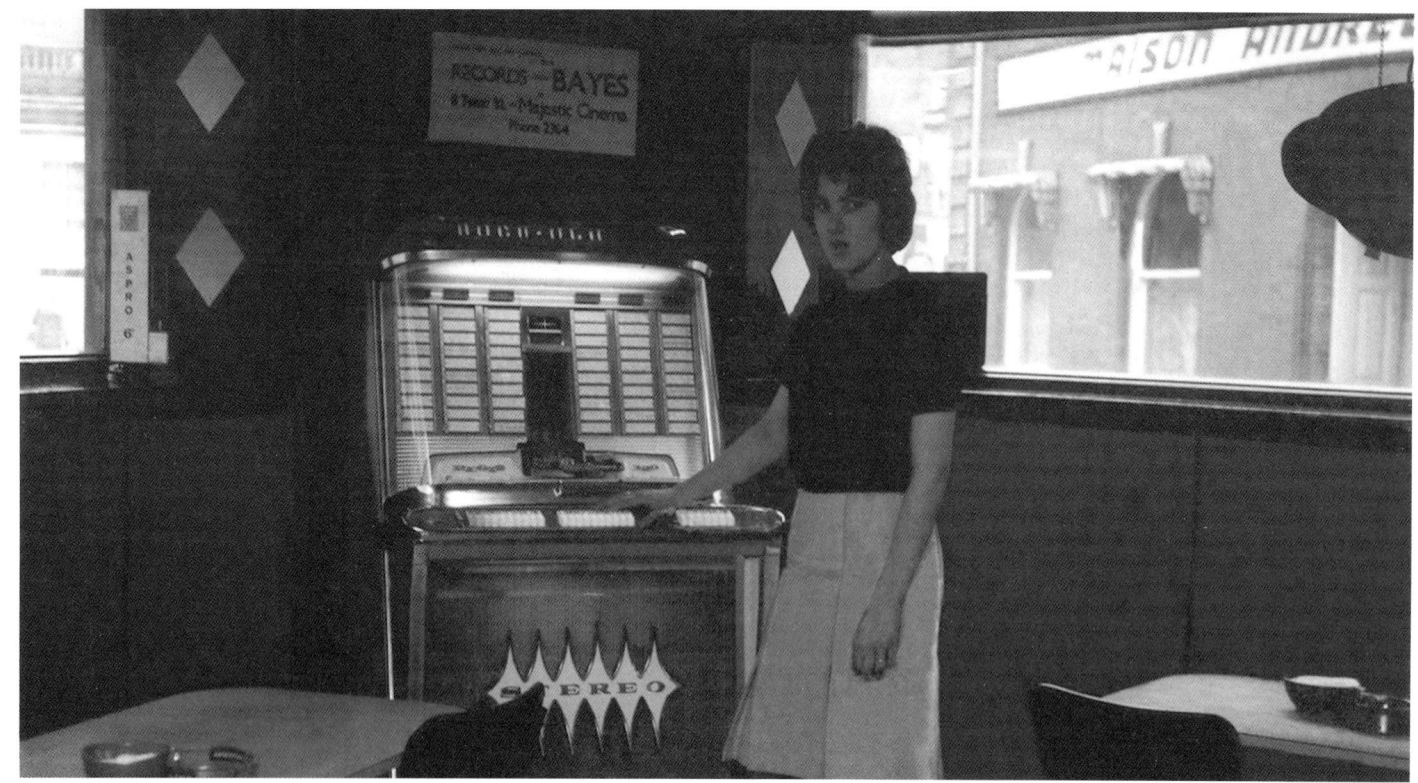

The 'Whisky', as it was known, is affectionately remembered by a certain generation.
TOP: Pauline Kingston stands by the 'Rock-ola' juke box in late 1963. The sign above advertises that Bayes supplies the records - it was my job to programme the box and to make sure that the Whisky was 'ahead of the trend'.
MIDDLE LEFT: Michael Griffin, Mel Wiles, Charlie Curtis & David Giles enjoy a chat and an Espresso.
MIDDLE RIGHT: Doreen Richardson with 'Whisky' - a stray cat that became the Whisky's resident feline!
BOTTOM LEFT: 'Tuffy' Warburton, Pauline Kingston, Doreen & Arthur Richardson.
BOTTOM RIGHT: 1971. A Lynn News photo shows the demolition - and the Whisky is just a fond memory.

Trouble in the High Street

TOP: In 1962 on a sunny afternoon the water main burst outside Woolworth's. The town beat 'bobby' directs traffic.

BOTTOM: In the early morning of 12th June 1968 a fire broke out on the first floor of the International Tea Co store at 42 High Street. It took firemen five hours to put the fire out. Stock to the value of £10,000 (at 1968 prices) was lost.

The Majestic in September 1963. This area is known as Baxter's Plain. Shops here include Wilfred Milton (butcher) on the left of the picture, Eve Rayner (ladies hairdresser) next to the Majestic and FJ Miles (chemist).

TOP: High above Tower Street Peter Todhunter and Ron Ess make safe the weather vane on the top of the Majestic in 1973.
LEFT: Jimmy and Jean Dawson's Book & Toy Shop in the shadow of the Majestic. Next door is FA Stone (tobacco and sweets).

BOTTOM LEFT: 1965. Looking down Tower Street with the Majestic on the left.
BOTTOM RIGHT: Peter and Ron struggle to remove the finial from the top of the vane.

TOP: Blackfriars Street in 1965, looking towards Stevens Corner - turning right here would bring one into St James Road.

ABOVE LEFT: St James' Road in about 1966, opposite the St James' Park, looking towards London Road. Just round the bend in the road was the Stanley Buildings. South Clough Lane is on the right - this lane ran parallel to Blackfriars Street.

ABOVE RIGHT: The Stanley Buildings (originally a library) became a canteen and kitchen for some primary schools in the area. In the picture, food is being prepared for a dinner.

LEFT: The Stanley Buildings pictured in circa 1906.

ABOVE LEFT: Whitefriars School fancy dress parade in 1970.

ABOVE RIGHT: 1972. St James Harvest Festival. The children had collected a variety of foodstuff for distribution by the St Raphael Club. *Left to right:* Angela Hall, Andrew Scott, Peter Child, Kim Twyman, Michael Day, Jane Dodds.

ABOVE: Gaywood Park Girls Class 1 Beta in 1960.
Back row (left to right): Bessie Barker, Jill Nurse, Susan Roper, Linda Wilson, Susan Benefer, Elizabeth Empson, Myrtle Massingham, Jean Faulker, Veronica Bowman, Brenda Harris.
Front row: Glynis Anderson, Joyce Louro, Janet Ess, Angela Warnes, Christine Fisher, June Mortimer, Christine Hare, Shirley Chestney, Eileen Dix.

LEFT: 1974. South Wootton Infants. *Standing & sitting in front of log (left to right):* Sarah Booth, Clare Bullock, Lisa Hobson, Belinda Albinson, Francesca Dodds, Helen Bowles.
Kneeling front: Jennifer Young, Maria Steward.

CLOCKWISE FROM TOP LEFT:
1) Old Time Dancing School, 1967.
2) Lynn News staff party, 1960.
3) Norwich City team members sign their record to celebrate promotion to Division One at Bayes Recordium, Tower Street, watched over by Mr & Mrs 'Bayes', in 1972.
4) The cast of Snow White, 1973/4.
5) The Mayoress, Mrs R Nurse, presents the winners of the under 17 five-a-side football KO cup final at the Corn Exchange in April 1964. M Futter, captain of YMCA Reds, holds the cup.
6) Jean Judge becomes Miss Pye TMC in 1974. She was presented with the sash at the Regis Rooms, Wellesley Street.
7) Modern Butter Packers Ladies Tug-O-War team (Carol Padget, Angela Cooper, Jean Faulkner, Tina Freeman & Eileen Dix) at the Walks in 1968.

ST. JAMES'S PRIMARY BOYS' SCHOOL

Of all the schools I attended I think St James was my favourite - the ingredients that made this school special were inspiring teaching and firm but fair discipline along with great friends.

TOP LEFT: In February 1974 Alan Fry shows the boys the way before a cross country training session. Alan had inspired the boys to try cross country and, thanks to his coaching, several had success at county level.

RIGHT: The team that won the English schools road race championship in 1974.

BOTTOM: 1973 St James Primary school. The school by now was becoming overcrowded - there were 329 pupils. Consequently the photographer could only get some of them in the picture.

By this time the school had an indoor heated swimming pool which had been paid for by funds raised by the pupils, parents and staff.

The area which included Wood Street & South Street was originally known as St James's End.
TOP LEFT: A winter's day in the 1960s looking down South Street.
ABOVE RIGHT: A woman walks up South Street to County Court Road.
LEFT: An old resident ponders on the derelict houses.
BELOW: County Court Road, looking north toward St James Park in the 1970s. Beyond the boarded up Spotted Cow is South Street and further down, Wood Street. Even further down next to the park was King's Lynn Corporation Depot - originally St James' Council School.
The Spotted Cow was the meeting place of the King's Lynn Cycling Club in the 1950s & 60s. Both South & Wood Street were hit by bombs in November 1940.

TOP: More than 100 Sunday School and Guide & Brownie packs met at the Tec in 1974. Between them they had collected more than £700 for the National Children's Home. The money was presented to the Mayoress of Lynn, Mrs Sidney Miller.

LEFT: A play group in 1969 at St Mary's Roman Catholic Infant's School in Church Lane (off All Saints Street) run by Mrs Angela Dewart.

BOTTOM LEFT: The Queen Mother arrives for the official opening of Whitefriars School in Whitefriars Road on 19th January 1971.

RIGHT: An open day at Whitefriars School in July 1970. Rosemary Huggins checks on the progress of Marie and Tracey.

TOP: Harry Southgate and his brother, Tom, pose outside his shop in 1974. A friend of mine took his girlfriend in to buy some tins of salmon when she brushed her leg against a sack of potatoes in the doorway. After my friend had made his purchase Harry casually said to him "how about buying your girlfriend a new pair of tights"!
BOTTOM: At 9/11 Loke Road was Misson's newsagent and general store. Mandy Smith waits to serve the next customer.

ABOVE: Mrs Dorothy Taylor weighs some bananas in her shop at 17, St James Street (RIGHT) in 1975. She had run the business on her own since her husband died in 1954. Her aunt and uncle (Mr & Mrs Dobson) ran a confectionery shop also in St James' Street. Her son, Richard, started work as a reporter for the Lynn News and was in the newspaper industry all his working life. Back in the late 1950s he had started the very popular 'Young Set' page in the Lynn News.

LEFT: 1968. The last year of trading for drapers Davy Bros at 19/20 Norfolk Street.
If you needed anything - millinery (women's hats), haberdashery (sewing items), buttons, or clothing (including boned corsets), then this was the place to go. It had been trading for nearly 70 years when it closed on 19th October 1968.

RIGHT: All Saints Street in 1967. The north side of the street has been bulldozed ready for the new Hillington Square. The grocery shop (at 33 All Saints Street), although run by Miss E Hare, retains the name Whitehand. The Whitehand family had been trading here since around 1900. The shop is now a private residence.

LEFT: The corner of South Clough Lane and Melbourne Street in Spring of 1969.
Before it closed a year or so earlier, it was listed as W Cawston (shopkeeper). This was a general store that mainly sold greengrocery. Before the war it had been a fish & chip shop. On the opposite corner was the Rose and Thistle (which I had wrongly named as the Rose and Crown in an earlier book - despite using the pub myself in the late 50s!).

The word 'clough' (pronounced as in plough) is derived from the Latin word *clusum* - meaning closed. In the Walks is a buried sluice (near the tennis courts) which linked the Purfleet watercourse to the Gaywood river. Since the river was the source of drinking water and the Purfleet was tidal it was necessary to stop the salt sea-water contaminating the drinking water so the sluice would be closed at high tides - hence the water course became known as the clough.

ABOVE: A showery Saturday in High Street on April 1957 doesn't deter the shoppers who had to be wary of traffic in the street. The Hovis and Café Imperial signs belong to Woodcocks (bakers).

BOTTOM Woodcock's Restaurant staff dinner in the early 1950s.

TOP: On 29th August 1971 High Street had been made permanently 'pedestrian only'. On the right of the picture is Dolcis (shoes), EDP offices, Purdy's (bakers & coffee bar), Burlinghams (jewellers) - next to Library Court which is still there today.
Across the street is Smith's (cleaners), Gallyon (gun maker) and Rivett's (ladies outfitters).

BOTTOM: New Conduit Street in July 1971. Now just a memory, this shopping development only lasted less than 30 years before it was torn down - to be replaced with more architecture not really in keeping with our small town.
The shops that can be seen are (*from left to right*): Scott & Son*, Hamlin (optician), Max Cards (greetings cards), Cavern Boutique, Roses Fashions, Peterborough Building Society, Keymarkets.
* Scott & Son had recently vacated their premises in High Street prior to demolition and taken out a very short lease here to sell their remaining stock.

TOP LEFT: Mountain Dew at the Fairstead pub in 1970. *Left to right*: John Cork, John Worfolk, Terry Rose, Les Wright.
TOP RIGHT: The Northern Quartet at the North Star, North Lynn in 1969.
Left to right: Ray Secker, Aubrey Harrod, Doug Briers, David Widdicombe.

MIDDLE LEFT: The Rhythmics dance band in the early 1950s. *Left to right:* Reg Smalls (trumpet), Bill Jones (tenor sax & trombone) - leader, Freddie Smith (drums), Ivan Dunbabin (alto sax), Jonnie Johnson (piano).
MIDDLE RIGHT: The Trojans at their second ever gig at Priory Hall, Priory Lane in 1961.
Left to right: Tony Mindham, Des Neville, Mike Williamson, Max Turner and Rod Shirley.

BOTTOM LEFT: The Geoff Stinton Band at the Dukes Head in 1968. *Left to right*: Mike Williamson, Geoff Stinton, Sheila Nash, Dave Raines, Rod Shirley, Mike Sherwood. After playing with other bands Geoff formed his own band in 1964. Owing to work commitments the band played it's final gig in 1978.
BOTTOM RIGHT: The Sabres outside the Youth Club in Tower Street in August 1964 after returning from Hamburg.*

Photo courtesy Rick Meek - from his excellent book 'Maids Head to Hamburg' - still available from local bookshops.

Starting at the TOP, the left-hand end of the Junior High School, King Street in 1971. The photo is spread over 2½ pages.

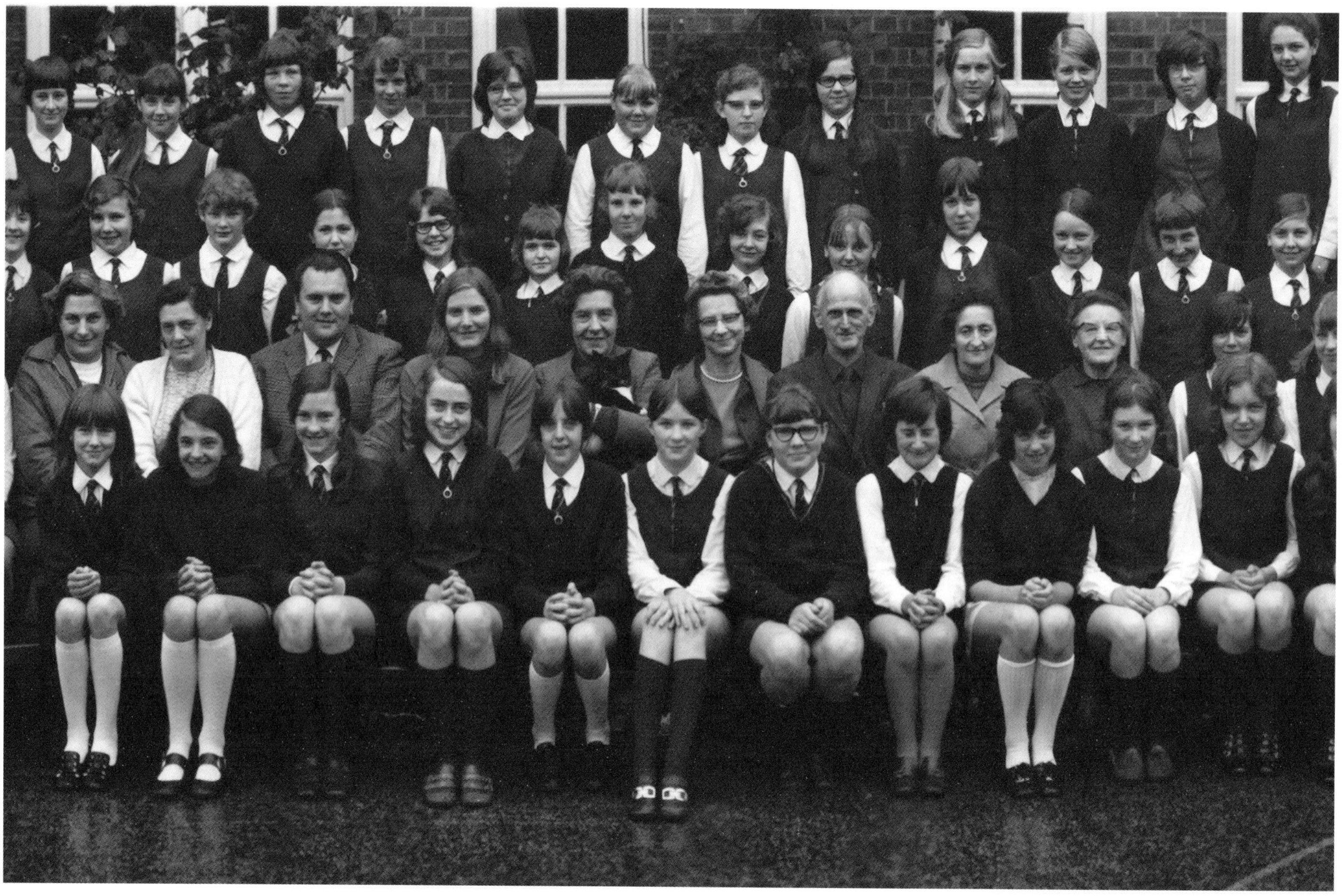

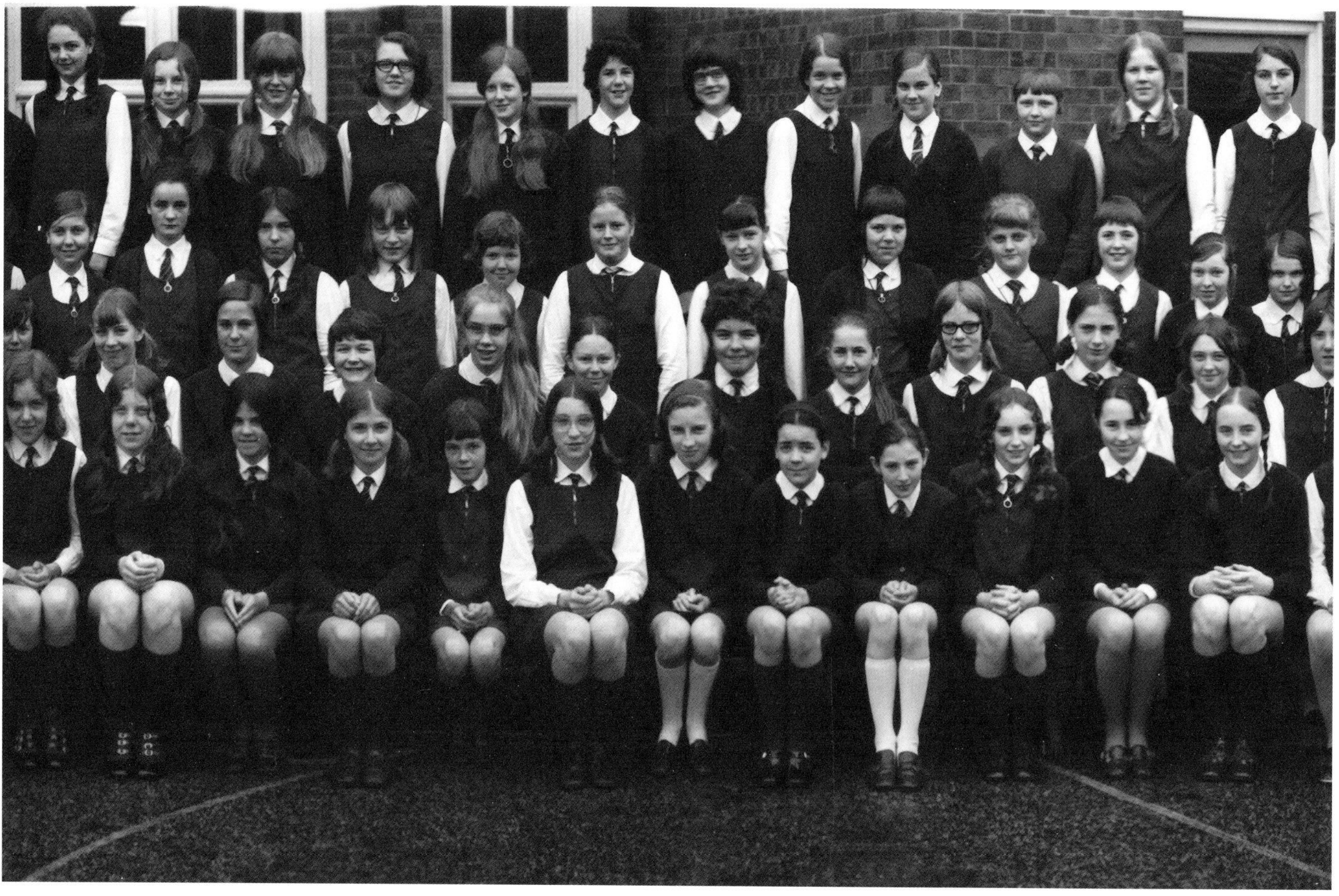

TOP: The right-hand end of the Junior High School long photo of 1971.

ABOVE: The High School Upper 6th form in 1967.
Back row (left to right): Barbara Wilcox, Margaret Bateman, Jeanette Herrick, Phrynne Howling, Anne Gillies, Pat Smith, Linda Gillies, Sheila Jarrett, Linda Coe, Ann Palmer, Patsi Turner, Pat Simper, Glynis Evans, Juliette Collison, Lynette Growcott, Margaret Whitehouse.
Middle row: Christine Merritt, Vivienne Easter, Margaret Tibbs, Mary Seaman, Pat Holmes, Veronica Bray, Pauline Appleton, Shirley Adcock, Valerie Skerry, Sandra Brancham, Lesley Bugg, Hilary Blomfield, Ruth Harrop, Jennifer Pottle, Penny Davey, Christine Marrington.
Front row: Angela Loades, Bridget Deans, Jane Petts, Valerie Jaggs, Gaynor Roby, Christine Gregg, Miss Fish, Lesley Thain, Penny Smylie, Diane Mutimer, Ann Copeman, Geraldine Kennedy, Margaret Howes.

TOP LEFT: The local government officers (NALGO) team in 1975. TOP RIGHT: Bayes Recordium football team of c1975.
ABOVE LEFT: Modern Butter Packers football team in 1969. ABOVE RIGHT: Bayes Recordium girl's football team c1975.

ABOVE: Lynn Regis boxers pose in their gym behind St George's Guildhall in 1958 after returning from Beccles where they won the Ronnie Ronalde cup. Ronnie Ronalde the whistling singer was very popular at the time and also a keen boxing supporter.

Back row (left to right): Jack Wadsley, Mick Hayes, ?, Peter Calton, Michael Kendal, ?, Larry Seaman.
Front row: Gerald Mallows, Mel Wiles, Charlie Curtis (holding the Ronnie Ronalde cup), Peter English, Alex Rudd.

TOP LEFT: Licensed Victualler's dinner at the Town Hall in the mid 1960s, Jack Cherrington (Rummer landlord), standing to the left is presiding. MP Derek Page sitting, with glasses, is guest of honour.
TOP RIGHT: 1972. WH Smith's staff at a party held at Peterborough. *Back row:* John Missing, David Mayfield, Philip Daws, Len Say, Ray & Veronica Stevens,?, ?, ?, Mr & Mrs Joe Ely. *Front row:* ?, ?, Mrs P Daws, Dot Say, Annette Croot, ?, Mrs D Mayfield.

LEFT: Lady members of the Conservative Club visit the Houses of Parliament in the early 1970s.

Ted Heath was the Prime Minister at the time - remembered for signing away our fishing waters and our entry into the EEC (now EU).

RIGHT: Members of the staff of Jermyn's assemble for a dinner at the Town Hall in the early 1960s. Jermyn's was originally established by Alfred Jermyn, later to become Jermyn and Perry's , then Jermyn & Sons and finally Debenham's in the early 1970s.

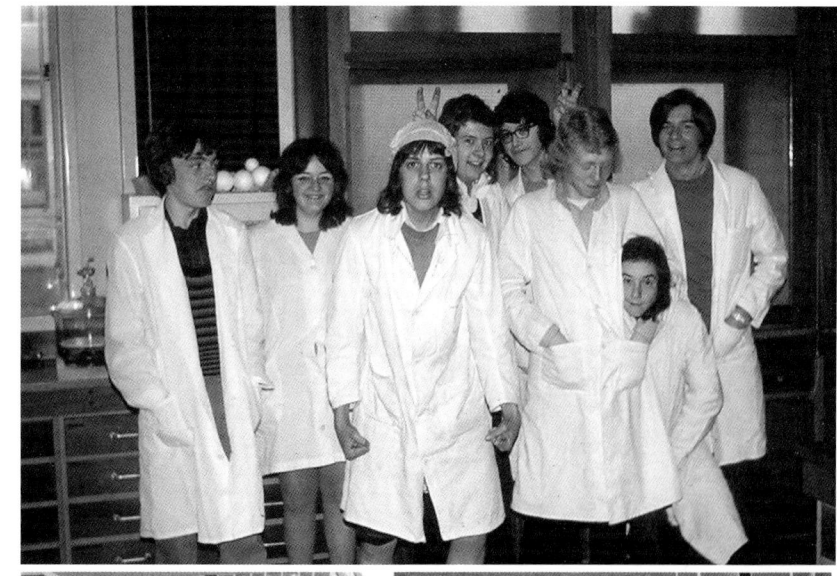

King's Lynn Technical College, County Technical College, Norfolk College of Arts and Technology were some of the names but it was just affectionately known as the 'Tec'.

TOP LEFT: 1973. The end of a chemistry practical exam for one of my groups - who relax in typical student fashion as I take a photo! This was virtually my last class after 11 years at the Tec - I had split my time between teaching and building up the record shop since 1962. In 1973 Janet and I took on a new shop unit in Broad Street as I had decided to concentrate on my first love - music.

MIDDLE LEFT: Some of the staff pose for a group photo in 1974.
TOP RIGHT: Engineering students at work in 1966.
UPPER MIDDLE RIGHT: Two of my fellow staff members, (Keith Simpkin (left) and Freddie Downton (right), are served lunch by a student in the staff dining room, watched by his tutor. As staff we were served up a superb three course meal, cooked by students, for 5/-.

ABOVE: A town carnival in 1963. Girls from the Tec passing down St James Street on their float - 'The old woman who lived in a shoe'.
Some of those in the picture include: Val Gordon, Jane Burch, Carol Berry, Tessa Thompson, Diane Glaysher, Monica Faulkner, Morag Bremner.
RIGHT:1967. A caricature of me drawn by one of my chemistry students - sometimes demonstrations could go spectacularly wrong! From the caption at least he knew what a pun was!

TOP LEFT:
In 1974 Ernie Dix bet he could walk from his pub in Snettisham to his work (the docks) in 2 hours. Here he is en route joined by the mayor, Eddie Edgley. Although he took 2½ hours he still raised £236 for the hospital children's unit.

TOP RIGHT: Ernie at work in the dock gate weighbridge office.

RIGHT: Sporting the latest fashion (hot pants) are the staff of Josephine's Hair Studio, 4, London Road in April 1971.
Left to right: Josephine Adderson, Rosemary Wilson, Jane Howard & Doreen Stevens.

LEFT:
Johnny's Tea Bar at the Cut Bridge, Wisbech Road in 1968.
John Rose had opened his tea bar in the late 1940s.
In 1968 with the impending demolition of the old cut bridge he had to close just short of 20 years serving tea to the travelling public - plus many locals.
Through this period all vehicles travelling to and from the Midlands & the North passed Johnny's.

ABOVE LEFT & RIGHT: A RAFA carnival procession travels down St James Street heading toward the Walks in 1961. The picture on the left shows a Royal Observer Corps group passing E Dennis & Son (butcher). To the left of the shop is part of St James' House. Here was the St James' Club and King's Lynn Conservative Club. At this time the Tec also used two rooms for classes.

LEFT: 1975. Another carnival procession passes the Police station en route to the Walks. This is a float entered by the Dairy Produce Packers - Queen Boadicea* (Dotty Seymour) and her soldiers.

Although from history lessons I don't recall Queen Boadicea's chariot driver wearing a suit, tie and cap!

*For the purists, now referred to as Queen Boudica (or Boudicca).

RIGHT & BELOW: In May 1960 Billy Smart's circus arrives in town at the station, with it's own dedicated train.
In the 1960s circuses were still very popular as proved by the large turnout to watch it arrive - complete with military band and animals. Also in the circus troupe was CoCo, the world famous clown, who also visited several schools to talk to the children about road safety.

£1m plan for Lynn marina

An aerial view of Lynn's Boal Quay (top of the picture) which is the centre of a £1 million marina project. The River Nar, seen winding its way into the Ouse, would have to be diverted to make way for a lagoon for 300 yachts. South Quay — not affected by the project — is seen at the bottom of the picture. (LC 4697)

'TIN POT PRESERVATIONISTS' ATTACKED
Battle between old and new

"TIN POT" preservationists are standing in the way of a scheme to build more homes for old people in the town, claims a Lynn councillor.

Mr. E. E. G. Edgley says the project would provide homes for more than thirty old folk in modern two-storey flatlets.

The snag is they would need to demolish six buildings in Southgate Street which are listed as "of architectural interest".

Councillor Eddie Edgley looks at the houses in Southgate Street, Lynn, which he thinks should be pulled down to make room for houses for old people. (LC 4076)

ALMOST a sight to give a hardened drinker apoplexy; the demolition of the former Barley Mow public house in Railway Road, Lynn. The building is being demolished to make way for the completion of the Old Sunway service road. (LC 6562).

'I detest the place'

As Seen in the Lynn News 1972
Clockwise from top left:

●DJ Alan Freeman opens the town's first night club, the Intercon.

●There's talk of a marina in the town - and nearly forty years on it's still just talk.

●The Barley Mow pub on Railway Road is pulled down to make way for Oldsunway access road.

●Young trainee journalist Malcolm Powell wins 'journalist of the year' - and he continued through hard work and determination to become Lynn News editor.

●In August Sir John Betjeman declares that "I detest the place" after he sees the awful architecture that is our new shopping precinct.

●A local councillor fails to agree that there is any "architectural interest" in some of our historical buildings - describing people who want to retain our heritage as "tin pot preservationists".
Others said that clearing the Coronation Square area and replacing the buildings with modern flats (Hillington Square) was the way forward.

Voted top journalist

"LYNN News and Advertiser" reporter Malcolm Powell (left) received a £60 cheque and medal from a director of the East Midland Allied Press Group, Mr. R. J. Winfrey, on Thursday.

Malcolm's award came after he was voted weekly newspaper journalist of the year and trainee journalist of the year in the EMAP group.

He faced competition from journalists on 17 other newspapers in the East Midland region.

Aged 20, Malcolm joined the "Lynn News and Advertiser" 18 months ago after attending King Edward VII Grammar School and Norfolk College of Arts and Technology.

ABOVE LEFT: Mr S.J.T Smith removes some freshly baked bread from the oven at his bakery in Lansdowne Street, North End in the mid 1970s.
ABOVE RIGHT: Steve Grange, Ivan English, Richard Adams and Bill Booth prepare for an exploratory dive in the dock in 1973.
BELOW: Bayes Recordium, Broad Street mid 1970s. Janice Cook and Oonah Tighe sort some new LP's out. Janet and I had moved from Tower Street in 1973 - taking on a 25 year lease (<u>upward</u> rent revision every 5 years - it usually more than doubled!).
It was a huge gamble and we could have lost everything but thanks to hard work, great staff and loyal customers we survived.

The South Gates, London Road on a damp sunny Sunday morning in early winter 1950. Note the slush on the road. Somehow Sunday mornings were special, in that there was always a quiet serenity with virtually no traffic, no shops open (except the odd newsagents), few people about and a Sunday dinner to look forward to - for some the highlight of the week!

A peaceful day for everyone to reflect and relax before work started on Monday.
Today one day blends into the next where the town hardly sleeps and no-one seems to have time to stop and enjoy peace and quiet.

The South Gates roundabout in 1963 - with the Southgate Services Ltd. (petrol filling station) and William H King (Ford main dealer) in the background.

TOP: The Millfleet where it joins the river in the late 1950s. On the left of the photo is SW Mitchley Ltd. (haulage contractors) which was situated on Boal Street[1]. Boal Street led from Bridge Street to the Boal Quay. The East Coast Steam Ship Co. Ltd. (shipowners, wharfingers & warehousing) is on the Boal Quay.

BOTTOM: A view in the opposite direction looking towards Morgan's Brewery and the Millfleet.

[1] In 1941 Boal Street was virtually completely destroyed along with serious damage inflicted on Bridge Street and Whitefriars Terrace. There were many fatalities.

TOP LEFT: Maid's Head, Tuesday Market Place in 1966. Colin & Mary Atkinson opened their new dance hall (a precursor to night clubs) which featured local and nationally well-known groups. Here, on the opening night, Mr & Mrs John Juby (Mayor and Mayoress) along with Colin and Mary, enjoy the opening evening.
ABOVE: The other pictures were taken by Pete and Mina Mott and show a fancy dress party in full swing (probably mid 1970s).

ABOVE: A party at the Vancouver Civic (or British) Restaurant*, New Conduit Street in 1951. This was organised by the drivers of British Road Services Haulage for their children.

MIDDLE RIGHT: The Workers Club Christmas dinner in the early 1950s at the Vancouver Civic Restaurant.

RIGHT: The Navy in Town. A dance at the (by then called) Tower Restaurant, New Conduit Street, in 1954.

*By the mid 1950s this pre-fabricated building had become the Tower Restaurant (during the war 'British restaurants' were common - offering a cheap meal for between 9^d and 1/6).
Eventually it was used by the High School as their canteen before it was demolished to make way for the new shopping centre.

Lincolnshire Canners Ltd (or Lin-can) Bankside, West Lynn.

TOP LEFT: Peas arrive at the factory for processing.

TOP RIGHT: Sorting the peas.

MIDDLE LEFT: After the cooking process. The canned peas are placed in large circular containers known as retorts. They are cooked at high temperature before being cooled and the tins labelled.

MIDDLE RIGHT: Boxing the canned peas up for despatch.

ABOVE: Children of the staff of Lin-can at a party in 1956.

RIGHT: A Lin-can staff party in 1962.

ABOVE: St Ann's Street looking towards St Ann's Fort in 1959. The bus stop is at No.14 St Ann's Street (Kerner-Greenwood - cement waterproofers). The large house is No.12. The property which is No.10 (next door) was about to be demolished.
This bus stop was on a route from the Millfleet to North Lynn via Chapel Street-St Ann's Street-Loke Road.
Another service to North Lynn ran via Gaywood Road to North Lynn. These two routes were classified the 38 & 38A services.

BOTTOM: Tuesday Market Place 1958.
Sir Vivian Fuchs carried out a successful Trans-Antarctic expedition. On show on the Tuesday Market Place was the Sno-Cat.

ABOVE: Circa 1959. A view of the bridge over the Nar on Wisbech Road. Across the river Eastern Gas is producing our gas but not for much longer. We would soon be using North Sea gas and the gasworks would be demolished. The gas being produced is obtained from coal or coke. As North Sea gas runs out and we still have plenty of coal maybe we should revert to building new gasworks and running them on 'clean' coal - I know this is not considered 'green' but until we come up with a perfect solution do we want to rely on gas imported from the East?

BOTTOM: It's September 1957 according to the calendar on the wall and Peter Graver sits in his office on the other side of the Nar at West Norfolk Fertilisers.
Peter Graver took the photo at the top of the page and many more in this book.

ABOVE: Tennyson Avenue crossing in 1959. Express engine 61623 (named Lambton Castle) departs with a train for Liverpool Street. You could wait here for a very long while, particularly when trucks were being shunted into the yard* - time seemed to stand still although walkers and bikers did have the option of using the footbridge.
* Shunting could also take place into the night - something the residents of Tennyson Avenue & Tennyson Road were resigned to!

BOTTOM:1968. But here time was moving rapidly on as the spectre of Hillington Square starts to take shape behind the scaffolding and the houses in front of the scaffolding on this side of the Millfleet await demolition. On the 'Fleet' the 39 bus waits to depart to South Wootton.

And Finally

Can you identify these less obvious locations around the town - all taken in the era of this book (1950 to 1975)?

Native Linnets should know at least 8 or 9! Our local experts will, of course, know them all.

104